A Product of a Pimp and a Prostitute

my forgiveness journey ...

A Product of a Pimp and a Prostitute

my forgiveness journey ...

a memoir by
CHARLES LISA

KING JESUS PRESS LLC

Copyright ©2018 by King Jesus Press LLC, Albany, New York
www.kingjesuspress.com

All rights reserved. Except as permitted under the U.S. Copyright Act of 1976, no part of this publication may be reproduced, distributed or transmitted in any form or by any means, or stored in a database or retrieval system, without the prior written permission of the publisher.

ISBN: 978-0-9998489-0-6 (Soft cover)
ISBN: 978-0-9998489-1-3 (E-book)
ISBN: 978-0-9998489-2-0 (Hard cover)

Library of Congress Control Number: 2018903160

Scripture quotations marked (KJV) are taken from The King James Version of the Bible, public domain.

Scripture taken from the New King James Version®. Copyright © 1982 by Thomas Nelson. Used by permission. All rights reserved.

THE HOLY BIBLE, NEW INTERNATIONAL VERSION®, NIV® Copyright © 1973, 1978, 1984, 2011 by Biblica, Inc.® Used by permission. All rights reserved worldwide.

Scripture quotations marked (NLT) are taken from the Holy Bible, New Living Translation, copyright ©1996, 2004, 2007, 2013, 2015 by Tyndale House Foundation. Used by permission of Tyndale House Publishers, Inc., Carol Stream, Illinois 60188. All rights reserved.

Author photo by: D'nique Productions
dniqueproductions.wix.com/dnique

DEDICATION

This book is dedicated to my family and to children across the world who have incarcerated or absent parents. May it lead you on a path to your own forgiveness journey.

In memory of my late Aunt Patricia Thompson who was looking forward to reading this book.
God called her home before it was published.

July 16, 1944 – September 4, 2017

CONTENTS

Foreword x

Introduction xii

Chapter 1: Call Me Mom! 2

Chapter 2: Where Does Your Mother Work? 8

Chapter 3: "The Talk" at 10 Years Old 18

Chapter 4: Mother's Day 26

Chapter 5: The Missing Fur 34

Chapter 6: Childhood Memories 44

Chapter 7: I Wasn't Doing That When I Was Your Age! 56

Chapter 8: Once a Thief, Always a Thief 66

Chapter 9: The Hole in the Ceiling 74

Chapter 10: The Letters 88

Chapter 11: The Gift of Forgiveness 104

Acknowledgments 136

About the Author 138

FOREWORD

Reading Charles Lisa's book, "A Product of a Pimp and a Prostitute", caused my mind to recall an incident that I read online. A father had taken his toddler daughter and wife to a baseball game and he had secured good seats in the front row along the foul line. I'm sure that the little girl was having a good time, not because she was attending a baseball game, but because she was with her daddy and mommy. Unbeknownst to this precious child a foul ball had been hit in their direction by the baseball player at bat. Her father jumped up to reach for the foul ball and, from the comfort of his lap, ejected the little girl and she tumbled to the ground. I felt so bad for this precious girl who was dropped by her father due to his pursuit of something "foul".

Sadly, her experience is a metaphor for the memories of many men and women. They know the pain of being dropped by persons who were supposed to love and protect them. They were dropped by an absentee father or a mother who was physically present but emotionally absent. This void of love and affirmation has caused many persons to go looking for love in all the wrong places, only to discover that there's a thin line between love and hate.

Fortunately, Charles Lisa has written about her story to bring healing and wholeness to your story. Her transparency, openness and inspiring narrative will bless all who read it. Be careful, you may have to deal with your issues and be challenged to let go of the past and reclaim your future. Beware, she challenges you to forgive yourself and others and not allow what has happened to you to block what God has for you. You can't change where you've been, but you can choose where you're going. This book is a game changer.

Dr. Damone Paul Johnson, Senior Pastor
Metropolitan New Testament Mission Baptist Church
Albany, NY and author of "A Life Worth Rebuilding"

INTRODUCTION

On Sunday, September 15, 1963, a bomb exploded at the 16th Street Baptist Church in Birmingham, Alabama, killing four innocent children attending Sunday School and hurting dozens of others. A sculpture in memory of the victims - Addie Mae Collins (age 14), Carol Denise McNair (age 11), Carole Robertson (age 14), and Cynthia Wesley (age 14) - stands in the park across the street from the church and reads, "A love that forgives". This phrase was the sermonic topic the Reverend John Cross, Jr., the church's pastor at that time, was going to preach the day of the bombing. How ironic, given the event that happened that day and the subsequent protests that led to more bloodshed!

In 2012, Jerry Sandusky was convicted of 45 counts of sexually abusing 10 young boys. Sandusky is a former Pennsylvania State University assistant football coach who also worked with troubled youth through a charity he founded. The repeated assaults against his victims occurred in his home, hotel rooms and on the college campus. One of his victims was one of his own adopted sons. How many men and women are living with the pain and emotional scars from sexual crimes that occurred in their childhood? Just like Sandusky's victims, how many of you have decided to trust that relative, neighbor, youth worker or family friend that offered gifts, money and attention, only to have that trust shattered?

Around 1970 - before I was even born - my maternal grandmother was home with her adult daughter, grandchildren and other house guests one day, when she was accidentally shot by her son-in-law with a shotgun. She was not the intended victim, but paid the price when she lost her left arm because of the incident. She did not lose her life, but as an amputee, she lost her income from not being able to work and had to learn to function with a missing limb. I wonder if she felt bitter every time she struggled to get dressed in the morning with one arm? Did she spew acrimonious words whenever cooking with one hand slowed her down? Or, when she drove her car steering differently than she did before she was shot?

Looking at these assorted stories of hate, hurt, abuse and violence, it is often difficult to find peace when you have experienced much pain. Even more, it is often challenging to forgive those who have perpetrated such offenses against us. Love is a great catalyst for change and is the basis for dealing with forgiveness. But, how can we have *"a love that forgives"* as the Rev. John Cross, Jr., was going to expound on in his 1963 sermon? With an act rooted in hate, how can we have the kind of love that forgives the men - known Klu Klux Klan members - who carried out such a horrific church bombing meant to terrorize the black community? Still affected by the trauma of being sexually abused as children, how can Sandusky's victims not feel angry every time they are haunted by bad memories? In a justice-driven world where there is no room for forgiveness, how could my grandmother have forgiven the man who disfigured her and altered her life for the remaining 30 years she had on this earth?

"A Product of a Pimp and a Prostitute" takes a hard look at this topic of forgiveness and the many facets it has. I address the "How can I forgive" questions head on, using my own forgiveness journey and the Bible as a guide.

There are two kinds of people in this world: those who are offenders and those who are offended. That means this topic is relevant to every single person breathing today because you have either experienced having to forgive someone for hurting you or you needed forgiveness for words or actions that have hurt someone. Perhaps, this is your current situation and not just merely a snapshot of your past. For some, this is a sensitive subject, as you might be struggling with deeply rooted and long-standing issues. Either way, this book is a useful tool to help you dissect your inner-most feelings surrounding forgiveness and confront them so you can finally have peace.

I wrote this book as a lengthy letter to my mother to open the lines of communication after nearly two decades of not speaking or seeing each other. I address so many life occurrences and a wide range of emotions I have experienced as I have dealt with her absence. We have had very little contact throughout the years due to her reoccurring time in prison, drug abuse and criminal lifestyle. Most of our communication have been letters she sent me from jail, some of which I still have.

In the first 10 chapters, you will read chronicles of my youth beginning with the first memories I have of my mother and the effects of her absence. Through my writing in these chapters, I hold a mirror up to my mother for her to see clearly the magnitude of her transgressions and the impact they have had on my life and others around her. I set the stage to address forgiveness in the final chapter by amplifying all her egregious mistakes first. By doing so, I hope she and other readers understand and appreciate the true meaning of grace. Grace is unmerited favor. You do nothing to earn it. It shows up when you extend to people those things they do not deserve. "For it is by grace you have been saved, through faith—and this is not from yourselves, it is the gift of God— not by works, so that no one can boast" (Ephesians 2:8-9 NIV). Once you *truly* appreciate God's grace, I guarantee it will be easier to extend grace to others who have wronged you and to demonstrate to them a love that forgives.

I pray this book brings healing to family members, friends, co-workers, church members and all others who read it. As you are reading, I hope you connect to my story in a relatable way. Whether you see yourselves in my mother or whether you see yourselves in me, please examine those relationships in your life that are broken because of unforgiveness and address them before it is too late.

Charles Lisa

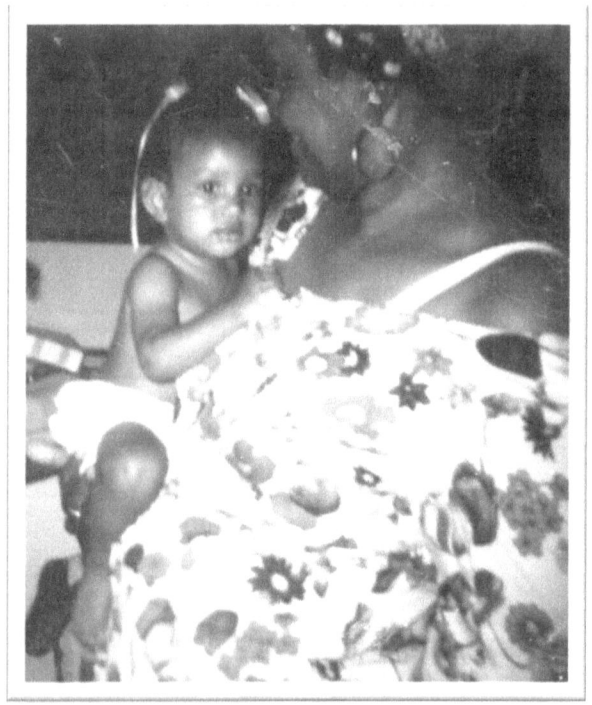

Chapter 1

Call Me Mom!

Dear Deborah,

Cousin Tracy and I were upstairs playing when we were called downstairs by that intimidating and commanding voice. As a child, those stairs seemed like they went on forever in that three-bedroom, two-story row house apartment facing the expressway. Looking back on my childhood home, I think the Maryner Homes was the best subsidized housing units I have ever seen! We had neatly manicured lawns and common areas that included sand boxes where I made mud pies and that good old-fashioned metal slide that burned my legs when the hot sun beat down on it.

From her favorite recliner, she yelled, "Get down here! I want to talk to you!" I was petrified every time I heard her stern voice. I thought I was in trouble whenever I heard her speak. I thought to myself, "What did I do this time?" Turns out, I wasn't in trouble at all. She just wanted to explain some things to us. "From now on, don't call me Grandma anymore. Every time we out in the stores, ya'll always sayin, 'Grandmaaaa,

Charles Lisa

Grandmaaaa'," explained your mother Hazel as she demonstrated how we would hold on to the "ma" and drag it out. I think it embarrassed her. "From now on," she said, "just call me Mom. And besides, I don't know where ya'll mamas are, and they ain't comin back for you no way!"

Wow! That was a lot to lay on two small children. I don't quite remember how old I was at the time. Somewhere between three and five years old I suppose. Tracy is two years older than me. Maybe she would remember. I don't think her sister Jackie was home at the time. Being nearly 10 years older than me, I'm sure Cousin Jackie was hanging out in the streets somewhere with her friends.

So, there we were. Three cousins living together as sisters because our mothers were nowhere to be found, being reared by a grandmother in a single-parent household where she didn't work. Little did I know at the time, that awkward moment, and that seemingly untraditional household, became the norm that stood commonplace in large numbers of black households.

I don't quite remember how I felt about what she said, but from then on, she was "Mom." The words, "Ya'll mamas ain't comin back for you" ordinarily would pierce anyone's heart, or at the very least sting. But like the saying goes – you can't miss what you've never had.

Call Me Mom!

Deborah, as the story was told to me, I was about six months old when Mom and Aunt Earlene scooped me up from the sofa I was lying on in some unsavory house where illicit activities took place. I don't know where you were but you weren't there with me. I don't even know who you left me with. But clearly, whoever alerted Mom to my whereabouts didn't feel like I was in the safest environment, so she came and rescued me. Mom took me home with her, and there I stayed until adulthood. So, the thought of you not coming back for me probably didn't bother me much... at the time.

I don't know how Jackie and Tracy came to live with Mom, but I'm sure it had something to do with neglect and abandonment by their mother as well. After all, Aunt Barbara didn't rear any of her five daughters.

My earliest memories of you are vague accounts of Mom and me boarding a Greyhound bus to visit you in jail. It was probably somewhere in Upstate New York where correctional facilities are everywhere.

Now that I'm grown, Deborah, I have so many questions for you, and I don't know where to start. I never understood how you could spend your entire life in and out of jail, locked up behind bars, being told what to eat, when to sleep and what to wear. Did you not understand the consequences of your actions? Or, did you think that you were so slick and so skilled at committing crimes that you wouldn't get caught?

Charles Lisa

Do you not enjoy freedom? How is it that you can feel like a human being when you have been caged for so long like an animal in the zoo?

Did you do drugs while I was in your womb? What led up to this path of darkness and self-destruction? Did you ever stop to think how your choices in life affected others, especially the child that you neglected and never cared for?

As promiscuous as you were when you were enjoying life out in the streets, how many times did you get pregnant? As far as I know, I'm the oldest, with David, Arlandria and Orlana trailing behind me, but did you have any other children that I don't know about? I do know about the son you had after David – Ortiz, who you left in the hospital and never went back for – but are there others? Do you ever wonder about Ortiz?

How many sexually-transmitted diseases have you had? I would find it hard to believe that you made it this far without contracting something! Are you HIV-positive? Do you have AIDS?

And, since you've spent so much time in close quarters with a bunch of other female convicts, have you ever slept with a woman? Are you gay? After all, your last prison stint was 15 years, and that is the stereotype of people in jail – men having sex with men; women having sex with women. It's not like you had access to the opposite sex. Well, there are the correctional officers but they don't count. Wait, have you ever been sexually assaulted by a correctional officer?! Heck, have you ever given in to their advances willingly?

I don't know. My knowledge of what goes on in those places is based on what I see on television, so if I sound a bit ignorant, well, that would be why. Blame it on cable TV. I just thank God I don't have first-hand knowledge of the penal system and that I didn't end up wasting so much of my life like you did!

Charles Lisa

Chapter 2

Where Does Your Mother Work?

One day on the school bus, my grammar school best friend, Omanda, asked me a dreaded question, "Where does your mother work?" Oftentimes, when people would ask me about my mother, I would get so confused. I didn't know if I was supposed to give a response about you or the woman that was caring for me. Either way, I was always saddened by the questions because I didn't know much about you and was too embarrassed to talk about my grandmother with the prosthetic arm who was unemployed.

Yes, as a child, it was uncomfortable to be reared by someone with a disability because of the ridicule from my peers. And besides, it was also embarrassing to be reared by someone who seemed so old! She wasn't one of the young, modern mothers like my other friends had. She was an old lady that wore old-fashioned clothes and funny looking wigs that all the kids were scared of because they all thought she was so mean. And they had good reason too. My friends couldn't call the house without being yelled at. If the street lights came on and I was not in the house, she would come looking for me with the extension cord in her hand ready to "tear my butt up" as she would say. I spent so much time stripping kitchen cabinets, laying down floor tile, cleaning the house, washing the Buick, on punishment or in the garden working like a farmer. I wanted to be outside playing dodgeball in the yard with my friends instead. Mom used to put the feet of rabbits and other small animals in her garden to keep the neighborhood kids from picking her beautifully-grown flowers and vegetables. She got them from her brother in Louisiana, whom everyone was afraid of because of the rumor he practiced voodoo! Who plants all sorts of flowers, tomatoes, peppers, collard greens, onions and cabbage in the projects anyway?

I know it sounds like I'm just taking a walk down memory lane, and in some ways, I am. But there is a point and a purpose to this letter, so bear with me as I reminisce.

When Omanda asked me, "Where does your mother work?" I answered, 'I don't think my mother works, but she has a lot of nice clothes!' At around nine years old, I didn't know what else to say. You always had some clothing items stored at our house in the coat closet downstairs or in the attic – beautiful dresses made of silk, snake skin shoes with the handbags to match, suede pants and more. Even as a child, I could tell they were expensive and made of the finest materials. As a matter of fact, I have pictures of you when you were all dressed up. You were cleaner than the Board of Health, as the saying goes! At this moment, I'm looking at a Polaroid of you in a white suit, black halter top that reveals your midriff and an elegant white hat adorned with feathers.

When you weren't in jail, there were times when you would come by the house, do a quick change, and then leave. I remember the stench of perfume mixed with funk when you walked through the door. It smelled as if you hadn't showered in days. Sometimes, you would even stay for a couple of days. You would sleep for what seemed like a week straight, put on a change of your fancy clothes and leave again. Really, that was the only time I ever saw you.

Being a more informed and less sheltered girl than I was, Omanda quickly told me that if you didn't have a job, but you could afford nice, fancy clothes, then you were a prostitute! I don't even know if I knew what that word meant at the time, but she must have discerned something in her short-lived but wise years, because as truth be told, she was right.

As a child, I saw you standing on the corners of Genesee Street or walking up and down Chippewa Street – areas in Buffalo that used to be known for prostitution and other criminal behavior. Sometimes, I think Mom drove down those streets intentionally to check up on you. I believe that was her assurance that you were still alive. See, a *good* parent shows concern for her children. She was keeping an eye on you even when you didn't realize it. A *good* parent also knows when to let go and let God handle the situation. Her proverbial hands might have been tied because it seemed like you were so far gone, but being the praying woman that she was, I'm sure she talked to God on your behalf.

Yes, over the years of my youth, I learned more and more about who you were – a career criminal who made her home in jail cells around the country, an addict who left me in the care of strangers, a prostitute who slept with men for money. The list goes on. My embarrassment of not fully knowing and having a relationship with you evolved into shame and melancholy as I learned more about you.

But what I do not know is, why? Why did you choose streets instead of schools? Why did you pursue a life of crime instead of a life of Christ? Why did you pick prostitution over purpose? Why did you prefer johns rather than jobs? Why did you accept violence over victory? And, why did you choose your drugs over your daughter?

Not only did I not have a mother, I didn't have a father either. The sad truth, though, is that there weren't any fathers around in our family. Statistically, this wasn't just the norm for our clan, but an overwhelming epidemic in our country as the result of teenage pregnancies, unwed mothers, and households plagued by divorce.

Prior to my 17th birthday, I only recall seeing my father, Chuckie, on about four occasions. The first time was

Where Does Your Mother Work?

when you took me over to his mother's house on Humboldt Parkway. Who knew that would be the only time I would ever see her. She was advanced in age, about 70 years old then, and she lived until she was 99. And if you want to shock a child, take her to her grandmother's house for the first time only for her to discover that her paternal grandmother is a white woman! "What? You mean to tell me I have white people in my family? I have white teachers, white classmates, and I even take communion every Sunday with white parishioners at Holy Cross Roman Catholic Church. But I didn't know my family members were white!" I thought to myself back then.

I saw Chuckie once when I was with him at someone's house where there was excessive gambling, drinking, cursing and smoking. I remember because the stench of the cigarette smoke was stifling. Even today, I can't stand to be around cigarette smoke. And the language! Although Mom used a few choice words in the house, there were definitely words that I never heard her say in all her 80 years on earth. The language pierced my tender ears because I wasn't used to that.

Then, there was the time I saw Chuckie at the store he and his father used to own. The array of penny candy in there is still etched in my brain (Yum!).

After that, I saw my father once when he came to our house in the Maryner Homes to see *you*. You just happened to be at our house. It was a Friday because that's when Mom would go out for her weekly card games. I was playing outside and decided to come in the house to look for my sweater. It got chilly outside, but I still wasn't ready to come in for good. I thought I left it in Mom's room. But when I went to retrieve it, do you remember what I saw? Mmmm hmmm – you and Chuckie in Mom's bed in a horizontal position! Yuk! I don't think I'll ever get the visual of walking in on my parents having sex out of my head! You yelled at me as if *I* did something wrong. But that wouldn't be the last time you would yell at me.

I had only known limited facts about my father. I knew his name was Charles (but everyone called him Chuckie) because you named me after him. I knew that he had more children than Abraham, the father of many nations. I knew the two of you were never married. And oh yeah, somewhere down the line, I learned that he was a pimp at one time. I'm not talking about the pimp that rappers talk about to hype their image or "wanna be" thugs brag about to gain street credit. He was the man who had ladies – excuse me – females on street corners chasing down johns for sexual transactions in exchange for money. He collected his pay and sent them back on the street to keep his enterprise afloat. He dressed them in sexy clothes and high heels. He owned women's bodies.

 Do you know how it feels to come to the realization that you are the product of a pimp and a prostitute?

Where Does Your Mother Work?

Did you two ever have a relationship, or was he just trying out the goods? Were you in love with him? Clearly, he had many women since he had 31 children, but were you his main one? I'm just trying to establish how you got to the point of having a child with a pimp.

The thought of talking about my parents growing up, and even in adulthood, made me want to slump down in my chair and disappear like they do in the cartoons. It reminds me of when I was in grammar school or even junior high and we would discuss slavery in history class. When we talked about this painful topic – one of the darkest times in American history – I used to feel disgusted, ashamed and worthless. I felt like all the white children in class were looking at me and forming an opinion about me based on my lineage. There wasn't anything positive that was ever said about slavery, blacks or the African diaspora, so for me, and I'm sure a great number of other blacks, I felt no sense of pride in my ancestry.

Likewise, growing up, I felt no sense of pride in the parents God chose for me. Like slavery, I thought that talking about my parents would make people form opinions about me. I thought people would judge me and think that I am less than. One of my fears as an adult was that someone would take me home to meet his parents and they would ask me about *my* parents. And once they found out the cloth that I was cut from, they would think I'm not good enough for their son.

Charles Lisa

This is my reality. This is the shame that hung over my head like a dark cloud on an overcast day. This, Deborah, is the result of your bad choices in life.

Charles Lisa

Chapter 3

"The Talk" at 10 Years Old

It was a quiet day and all seemed calm until I was summoned into the living room where Mom sat in her favorite recliner. If she wasn't upstairs in her bed watching television, she was downstairs in that recliner with one leg hanging off the arm of the chair! She was reading the mail she just retrieved from the mailbox. There was one letter of interest to her that she felt was important enough to share the contents with me. She had that serious face. "Here we go," I thought.

Apparently, the letter was from either you writing from jail, or the court system with a letter addressed to you. I don't remember which, but I do remember your name was nowhere on the envelope. Instead, my name – my full government name – stood where yours should have!

Mom explained to me as best as she knew how, that you got into trouble yet again, but this time you gave the police officers my name! She sat me down to explain to me how one day, I might be questioned about this crime that I allegedly committed, and I should explain that it was my mother who used my name illegally. She also said that I should point out the date of birth to prove that it could not have possibly been me, this 10-year-old kid, who was accused or convicted of breaking the law. Apparently, my name wasn't the only one you had used over the years to mask your true identity. In January 1997, you were Veronica Hall. In December 1998, you were Larsena Little. Then there was Deborah Morris. These are just the ones I know about. Who knows how many other aliases you've used over the years to evade getting caught or to steal someone else's identity!

I'm not sure who I would have to explain this to. The police? A judge? A future employer? My future husband? I was equipped because Mom prepared me, but I should have never been put in a position of worrying about whether or not I was going to be in trouble for a crime you committed. Who does that to their child, someone you're supposed to love and protect? You seriously had no problem making the decision to ruin my good name to save yourself? I honestly lived with the fear that I could possibly do jail time because of you. But, then I remembered Scripture: **"I will fear no evil"**!

Around this same time in my life, Mom handed me a Bible. It looked like one of those Bibles they used to have in hotel rooms on the night stand. I don't know if they still provide Bibles in hotel rooms anymore. I have been in hotels and resorts around the world, and I don't know the last time I've seen one.

"The Talk" at 10 Years Old

Reading the Bible wasn't a strange phenomenon for me. After all, Mom made sure I had the best education I could possibly get by sending me to a Catholic school. There, religion class was as normal as math and history. I learned the Model Prayer, the 10 Commandments and the Beatitudes. I learned that stealing, lying, fornication and adultery were wrong – all those traits you possessed. I learned discipline, and while you were defying authority, I learned respect for authority. My faith was strengthened, and I gained knowledge and understanding of Jesus Christ. I attended Mass every Sunday. The teachings I learned in school were reinforced at church. Even though Mom did not attend church, she knew the importance of it, and she also reinforced Christian principles at home. So, when Mom handed me that Bible, it wasn't new to me.

Mom didn't just hand me the Bible. She took it one step further. She opened it to the Old Testament, Psalm 23, and said, "Here, learn this." That was all she said before she walked away. She didn't always use a bunch of words to make a point. She didn't have to be an eloquent orator or recite a monologue to get attention. She didn't even use good grammar, being an uneducated woman from the South. Her actions were strong though, and her commandments were to be followed. So, what did I do? I learned Psalm 23... immediately!

> The LORD is my shepherd, I lack nothing.
> [2] He makes me lie down in green pastures,

he leads me beside quiet waters,
³ he refreshes my soul.
He guides me along the right paths
   for his name's sake.
⁴ Even though I walk
   through the darkest valley,
I will fear no evil,
   for you are with me;
your rod and your staff,
   they comfort me.
⁵ You prepare a table before me
   in the presence of my enemies.
You anoint my head with oil;
   my cup overflows.
⁶ Surely your goodness and love will follow me
   all the days of my life,
and I will dwell in the house of the LORD
   forever. (NIV)

Even today, when I think about the 23rd Psalm, I think of Mom. See, by learning this Scripture, I knew that I no longer had to fear getting into trouble for *your* transgressions. The 4th verse tells me so! As long as the LORD was guiding me along the right path, even in dreary days, dark nights, abandonment, lonely hearts, wicked schemes, lying tongues and disappointing parents, I didn't have to be afraid! I had goodness and love on my side! I had mercy in my corner!

Not only was I memorizing Scripture and hiding them in my heart, but I began to have a consistent and voracious appetite for prayer. Of course, we prayed in school every day, but I prayed at night before bedtime,

"The Talk" at 10 Years Old

and during the day, whenever there was a need. It seemed like my prayers went on for hours! This is when I began praying for you, even though I did not like your ways.

I recall learning in school about a man in the Bible named Saul. Saul was a man full of hate. He was a sinful man who had no regard for truth, goodness or love. Saul did not believe in Jesus Christ, and he imprisoned and even killed anyone who professed Christ. Saul had a bounty on the heads of all the LORD's disciples. Man or woman, he didn't care. He set out to destroy the church body, and he went from house to house dragging people off to jail because of their beliefs. I thought, "Wow, this man is horrible!"

Then, Jesus began to work on Saul. First, He called Saul out by name and confronted him about his actions. He accosted Saul on the street and asked him why he was persecuting Him. See, every time Saul pursued, harassed and oppressed Christians, he was persecuting Jesus Christ all over again.

At that moment, Saul recognized Christ for who He was, and it was at that moment when his inward transformation began.

After Jesus blinded Saul for three days and orchestrated the restoration of his sight, he became a believer. He began praying, fasting, spending time with other disciples, and going from city to city telling everyone about Jesus Christ. God changed Saul's name to Paul, and he became one of the greatest leaders highlighted in the Bible.

I used to think about you when I learned about Saul in school. I thought, "Wow, if God could forgive a murderer like Saul who scandalized His name at every turn and who did such heinous acts against Him, use him to spread Christianity throughout the world and allow him to author 13 out of the 27 books in the New Testament of the Bible, surely, He could change my mother and use her life for greatness!"

As such, my prayer as a little girl was for God to transform your life like He did Saul's. My prayer today remains the same.

I had enough faith back then to believe God was able to do just that. I knew He would do it someday, in His time.

Charles Lisa

Chapter 4

Mother's Day

In 1908, a woman named Anna Jarvis first celebrated Mother's Day in the United States as an occasion for honoring the sacrifices individual mothers made for their children. She then began a campaign to make Mother's Day a recognized holiday in this country. President Woodrow Wilson made Mother's Day an official holiday in 1914. And today, more than a century later, we celebrate mothers, motherhood and maternal bonds every year in May.

There was a Mother's Day that I remember vividly. I was a little girl, and you came by our house on a Saturday to spend the night. Sunday morning came, and I got up for church like any other Sunday. When I got home, I did what came naturally; I gave Mom her Mother's Day card I made.

Well, I recall you screaming at the top of your lungs at me because I did not have a Mother's Day card for you. You were insulted, angry and, I suppose, hurt because I recognized my grandmother who was feeding me, clothing me, educating me, teaching me, caring for me, providing for me, sheltering me, and praying for me, rather than recognizing you.

Charles Lisa

You felt left out because of all the things you did for me…wait… what did you ever do for me that would warrant recognition on Mother's Day?

Did you ever instill any values in me? Did you ever take me to any doctor's appointments or care for me when I got sick? Did you teach me my alphabet or tutor me in math when I was having difficulties learning it? Did you ever contribute to my school tuition that Mom struggled to pay just so I could have a good education? Did you ever teach me how to sew? Did you ever teach me how to braid my hair or stop me from putting damaging chemicals in my hair to straighten it and encourage me to embrace my beautiful, natural tresses? Did you give me words of affirmation when I felt like an awkward kid? Did you ever make me feel beautiful when everyone else made me feel like something was wrong with me for being "so skinny"? Did you ever protect me when the jealous girls in the neighborhood wanted to fight me or when I was taunted right in my own home by my older cousins? Did you ever spend quality time with me by playing board games or taking me to the movies? Did you ever teach me how to garden? Did you ever open a savings account for me or teach me about money management? Did you ever show me how to put on make-up? Did you ever teach me how to cook anything? Did you ever tuck me into bed at night? Did you ever teach me how to swallow pills? Did you ever teach me how to dance? Did you make it to any of my softball games or school plays?

Mother's Day

Did you ever come to church and listen to me sing in the choir or attend my First Communion? Did you ever accompany me on any school fieldtrips? Did you ever buy me a pair of tights to wear under my school uniform in Buffalo's harsh winters? Did you ever take me fishing? Did you ever teach me any card games? Did you ever give me a heart-shaped box of chocolates for Valentine's Day? Did you ever dye Easter eggs with me? Did you ever take me on a vacation? Did you ever help guide me in a career path? Did you ever teach me pride in my African roots? Did you ever attend any of my school graduations? Did you ever explain to me that someday, by God's design, I would go through a menstrual cycle every month and it's nothing to be ashamed of? Did you ever show me how to use tampons or what to do when I would bleed through my clothes during heavy periods? Did you ever school me on what types of boys to date and what type of man I should marry? Did you ever warn me that men will try to prey on me or teach me how to not fall victim to them? Did you ever talk to me about sex? Did you ever show me how to be a lady?

You and I both know the answer to these questions, Deborah. So why in the world would you expect me to think about you enough on Mother's Day to give you a card?

What's interesting, when I gave Mom her card, the thought never crossed my mind to give you one too.

Charles Lisa

Frankly, you were present that day, but it didn't warrant any presents from me!

But you stood there towering over and yelling at me, trying to make me feel guilty about not thinking about you, someone I saw only on occasion.

I think you, and so many other mothers out there, have this concept of Mother's Day all wrong. See, when Anna Jarvis conceptualized this idea, it wasn't about a general celebration of all the women who gave birth. Let's face it, any animal can have babies! It was about what individual mothers meant to their children, based on all they've done in the lives of their children, and children showing their appreciation for this. As a matter of fact, Anna Jarvis intentionally used apostrophe "s" (Mother's Day) instead of "s" apostrophe (Mothers' Day) to illustrate her concept. The first refers to one mother and the latter refers to more than one mother. It was always meant to be a personal celebration between mothers and families.

So, after all your fussing and finger wagging, what did I do? You shamed me into taking that long walk up to Rite Aid where I purchased a card just to shut you up. I hope that the store-bought card I came back home with made you feel like a mother, if only for one day!

Anna Jarvis' version of Mother's Day involved wearing a white carnation as a badge and visiting one's mother or attending church services. Today, the tradition has

Mother's Day

expanded where people wear red carnations on Mother's Day if their mother is still alive – white carnations if their mother is deceased. Since May 1999, the first Mother's Day since Mom's passing, I have requested a white carnation at church for those that give out flowers during service on Mother's Day.

I have been told many stories by the elders growing up, and my favorite great uncle in Louisiana told me a story about how you and Mom were in Louisiana visiting one summer when I was a baby, and you got upset about something and stormed off to the bus station to get home on your own. Uncle said he followed you because I was with you, and he wanted to make sure I was safe. He told me you passed by a trash can while you were walking through the bus station and threw me in; this little baby who was all wrapped up in a blanket! He said he pulled me out of the trash, and he never lets me forget it! Even today, he still tells me this story, "You know I pulled you out of the garbage can when Lonesome Road threw you in, right?" Lonesome Road is his nickname for you!

At first, I thought he was just joking because it sounds far-fetched that you or anyone else would do something like that. But, in his advanced age, he still sticks by this story today, although I'm sure you will deny these actions.

But, you throwing me into a bus station trash can is no more far-fetched than Amy Woodard-Davis being thrown into the trash then burned by her mother a few decades ago when she was a few hours old; or Susan Smith drowning her two young sons in 1994, buckling them into their car seats and pushing the car into a South Carolina lake; or Andrea Yates drowning her five children in the bathtub in their Houston home in 2001; or China Arnold killing her three-week-old daughter in a microwave oven in Dayton, Ohio, in 2005!

Yes, this type of abuse, neglect and harm isn't far-fetched at all. It's the reality that, unfortunately, so many children in this country face.

I do not know what the outcome would have been if my uncle wasn't trailing behind you. I also do not know the reason behind your actions. But I do know that the woman who allegedly threw me in a bus station trash can when I was a baby was the same woman who demanded a Mother's Day card from me some years later.

Theft of Coat Leads To Woman's Arrest

A woman accused of breaking into a Maryner Homes apartment and taking a $2,500 mink coat in August was arrested today on several warrants.

Detectives Angelo Martinelli and Joel Scime of the Special Frauds Bureau arrested Deborah L. Encarnacion, 29, of Maryner Homes on charges of burglary and grand larceny. She also faces charges of issuing a bad check, grand larceny and violating probation, police said.

Buffalo News – Circa September 1982

Chapter 5

The Missing Fur

One of my fondest memories from my childhood was taking family vacations. Every year, first week in August, Mom would load up the car, stock up on her eight-tracks and cassette tapes, and drive us to her home state, Louisiana. Blues was her music genre of choice, and BB King kept us company the entire way. It was a long, 24-hour car ride through the South, but it sure was fun as a child!

Before the trip, we would stop by Papa's house, and he would hand me a piece of aluminum foil folded up. He would say, "Sugar Bear, don't open it until you reach the Pennsylvania border!" Sugar Bear was the name he affectionately called me. As soon as we hit the toll booth crossing into Pennsylvania, I would open that foil and find a 20-dollar bill! It was like Christmas! Papa always made sure we had traveling money to buy snacks on the road or trinkets along the way. And even though Mom and Papa were separated and living their lives apart from one another, they still took care of each other.

Sometimes, we would take a detour to Uniontown, Alabama, before making our way to Baton Rouge. There, we would stop by Aunt Bertha's farm. I loved seeing her pigs, roosters, chickens, cows and horses! Her yard was also sprawling with pear, fig and pecan trees. I always left there with a shopping bag full of pears that I picked, even though they were not ripe yet!

Aunt Bertha wasn't really related to us, but Mom made sure we used titles like aunt, miss or mister to refer to all our elders. And, because Mom used to date Aunt Bertha's brother, Grandpa Sleepy, she was like an auntie to us.

While we embarked on an annual trip down South one year, you were up to your old tricks as usual. You knew our vacation schedule since it did not change from year to year, and you took that as an opportunity to burglarize our home. Grandpa Sleepy was house sitting while we were away and served as witness to your crimes.

I recall him retelling the story to Mom upon our return. "Who down there?" Grandpa Sleepy yelled out from upstairs as he heard you enter the house. "Who up there?" you returned the questioning. That line became a running joke in our family after the dust settled!

But Deborah, your crime was no laughing matter. Not only did you break into our home, you also escaped with Mom's fabulous mink coat! You were a determined thief, and the fact that Grandpa Sleepy was there did not deter you from stealing from your mother.

The Missing Fur

I imagine it did not come easy for Mom to acquire a luxury item like that valued at $2,500. It's not like we were rich! This was a beautiful, three-quarter-length mink coat monogrammed with her initials inside. I'm not sure where she got it from but, like all her possessions, she took good care of it. Oftentimes, when winter season ended, Mom would have her fur professionally cleaned and stored at a temperature-controlled facility to preserve it. I'm not sure why she chose not to store it properly this time around, leaving it vulnerable to theft!

I can imagine the hurt Mom felt from her own flesh and blood – her youngest daughter – robbing her. Well, her hurt must have turned into anger and a pursuit for justice because she pressed charges against you. And rightfully so … you committed a crime!

All these years, I held on to the newspaper clipping where the news of your arrest for burglary and theft was publicized. According to the article, you were also wanted on some other unrelated charges: issuing bad checks, grand larceny (Mom wasn't the first person you ripped off!) and violating probation. It was not very smart to commit crimes while you were already wanted on other charges! Mom pointed the article out to me when it appeared in the *Buffalo News*, and I took it upon myself to clip it out of the paper and save it. I'm not sure why I decided to do that at the time, but your crime against your family is forever memorialized in this article.

Grandpa Sleepy eventually had to go to court to testify against you. He was so upset because he lost a day of wages at the factory where he worked and nothing to show for it. He was serious about his work attendance, and he vowed never to stick his nose into other people's business again.

Mom was determined to get her coat back, with or without the help of the police. She eventually did, retrieving it from the house where you stashed it. It's a good thing she got to it before you had a chance to sell it. Exchanging this family heirloom for a measly dollar equivalent to a fraction of the cost she paid for it would have just bankrolled your drug habit for a few more days.

It was so important to you that I treated *you* like a mother. However, you showed *your* mother little respect. You used to enjoy writing letters from prison talking about how you're saved now and preaching and quoting Scripture like Exodus 20:12, "Honor your father and your mother, that your days may be long upon the land which the Lord your God is giving you." It seems like you lived by the, "do as I say, not as I do" rule.

Why is it that when people go to prison, they suddenly start practicing jail-house religion? Don't get me wrong, I know the power of the Holy Spirit, and I know God can save people where ever they are. However, when you gravitate to the Bible to comfort you temporarily while you're confined, then you wreak all kinds of havoc and turn your back on God as soon as you get out, it makes me wonder if your salvation is authentic.

So, while you were thumbing through the Bible looking up Scripture that you could use to intimidate me from behind bars, did you happen to run across:

"But be doers of the word, and not hearers only, deceiving yourselves." – **James 1:22 NKJV** – You should have incorporated this one when you were advising me to honor you but you neglected to honor your own mother!

"You shall not take the name of the LORD your God in vain, for the LORD will not hold him guiltless who takes His name in vain." – **Exodus 20:7 NKJV** – How many times did you cuss someone out, including me, using God's name in combination with a bad word?

"You shall not commit adultery." – **Exodus 20:14 NKJV** – How many of the men you slept with for money were married?

"You shall not steal." – **Exodus 20:15 NKJV** – Your rap sheet indicates you have neglected this commandment all your life!

"You shall not bear false witness against your neighbor." – **Exodus 20:16 NKJV** – I'm sure that really wasn't Larsena Little or Veronica Hall in jail!

*"You shall not covet your neighbor's house; you shall not covet your neighbor's wife, nor his male servant, nor his female servant, nor his ox, nor his donkey, nor

anything that is your neighbor's." – **Exodus 20:17 NKJV** – Or your neighbor's fur coat!

"But fornication and all uncleanness or covetousness, let it not even be named among you, as is fitting for saints." – **Ephesians 5:3 NKJV** – Prostitution is fornication!

"Therefore, if anyone is in Christ, he is a new creation; old things have passed away; behold, all things have become new." - **II Corinthians 5:17 NKJV** – When you say you are saved, don't you know there should be some evidence of that, like not continuing your life of crime and deception?

Before Mom died on October 23, 1998, she left me instructions on what she wanted me to do with all her possessions. I continued to hold on to her prized mink coat, just as she instructed. Even though it was too big for me to wear, I kept it anyway.

Since the coat was a family heirloom, I let a family member borrow it one day. I introduced my big cousin to the life of politics where I used to attend many galas, fundraisers and other political events. She accompanied me one weekend to the New York State Black, Puerto Rican, Hispanic and Asian Legislative Caucus in Albany. This was an annual premier event for the who's who in politics for people of color. All the ladies were decked out in their full-length fabulous furs for this fancy affair. Not only were they stylish, but practical as well since

The Missing Fur

Caucus weekend took place in what always seemed like the coldest weekend in February!

I wore another fur coat that I have, and I wanted my cousin to fit in with everyone else so I let her wear Mom's mink. I was hesitant because she is a smoker and I did not want it coming back to me with the stench of cigarette smoke.

I let my cousin borrow the coat, with the clear intention that she was supposed to give it back, but I guess she had other plans. For months, I would ask her to return it, but to no avail. Nine months later, I moved out of New York and went to Georgia. I visited her the day before I was moving, and I told her to get the coat out of the closet so I would not forget to take it with me. But, of course, she did not. I ended up leaving there without the coat, and I knew my chances of getting it back from her were slim.

Years later, even while I was living in Georgia, I would plead with her to return the coat. She even got nasty with me about it saying, "Why do you keep sweating me about this coat? Is it that cold in Georgia?" How does one get upset when one is asked to return something one borrowed? Who does that?

I pleaded one last time for her to return the coat. I guess she figured she'd shut me up for good by telling me the coat was destroyed. She claimed that she had it in a garbage bag in the basement, and the basement flooded, thus destroying the coat. I guess she forgot about the other lie she told me previously, because according to her, she left the coat in her apartment in the Bronx before moving back to Buffalo because she had no more room to transport anything else. Who moves a house full of junk, but leaves a valuable heirloom behind? And who takes a $2,500 mink coat, stuffs it in a garbage bag, then throws it in a basement filled with mildew?

I had foreknowledge that my cousin wasn't a truthful or ethical person, so her actions did not surprise me. I do not know the truth about the coat. It would not surprise me if she sold it for $5 at a flea market or if she is still wearing it until this day. But, the outcome is that I will never see it again. The coat Mom fought so hard to get back after you stole it is gone forever. It is shameful that the tales of this coat are encased in theft and deception at the hands of family members – the two family members that she trusted the least. Mom always said that my big cousin was messy and that you were no good.

Charles Lisa

Chapter 6

Childhood Memories

I asked a few people to share with me their fondest memories of their mothers. One person told me his fondest memories were watching television programs like "The Gong Show" with his mother when he was a child. For him, it was a sense of comfort. It was peaceful. It was security knowing his mother was there. He recalled his mother helping him read and do homework. She was big on academics. He marveled at her cooking, as if he could still smell the aroma of West Indian food simmering on the stove. She was always cooking – never missed a meal. Dinner was ready at the same time every day. He recounted having fond memories of her personality – lively; loved to dance; loved to entertain; selfless.

The other person told me her fondest memories with her mother as a child was taking family vacations to exotic destinations like Puerto Rico and Jamaica. She absolutely enjoyed going to beaches, and the Caribbean Sea was breathtaking. They weren't the kinds of vacations her other friends experienced at that age, if they even went on vacations at all. Her mother would also wake her up in the morning as a child with a silly routine of stretching their arms to the sky and reciting, "yawwwwwn and streeeetchhhhhh, yawwwwwn and streeeetchhhhhh." Then, there were the rematches of Candy Land, everyone's favorite childhood board game, that they played over and over.

Missing Money

Me? Well, Deborah, I'm drawing a blank as I try to recount fond memories of *you* growing up. I'll tell you what I do remember though.

My "play cousin" and I used to save up our change whenever we would get money. Mom didn't give me an allowance, but I did get money from Papa whenever I would go to his house and help him clean. Then, there was my occasional Kool-Aid and popcorn stand where I made a few coins along the way by selling refreshing treats to the neighborhood kids.

We kept our savings in a jar at my house where it rested "safely" on my dresser. This was our movie fund, so the next time we pleaded with someone to take us to the movies, we wouldn't be rejected for monetary reasons.

After your departure from one of your brief visits, I noticed the money in the jar disappeared. We were two little girls, not working teens, so it was devastating to find out that the money we scrimped and saved was gone! "It would take forever to replenish it!" I thought.

Saddened, I made my way into Mom's room and told her what I suspected – that *you* stole our money out of the jar.

Childhood Memories

Mom must have confronted you with this news, because the next time you came over, you voiced your displeasure with my accusation. That's putting it mildly!

As you wagged that index finger in my face with the sharp, long fingernail polished in a hue of red, you hemmed me up against the wall in the living room and scolded me for lying on you.

"DID YOU SEE ME TAKE IT? DID YOU SEE ME TAKE IT?" You kept yelling. As you stood there towering over me, standing as close as you could get with one hand around the collar of my shirt and the other one in my face, Mom just sat there in her recliner and didn't say a word. "Why is she just sitting there allowing her to torment me like this?" I thought. I looked for her to come to my rescue, but to no avail. All I could do is stand there and cry while you played the victim role and treated me like *I* was a criminal. You were right. I didn't see you take it. But when you have a reputation for theft, you shouldn't be surprised when accusatory fingers are pointed at you.

Cop Career

At one point in my childhood, I told Mom I wanted to be a police officer when I grew up. It wasn't because I was fascinated with guns. It wasn't because of the respect that came with the uniform. It wasn't because I wanted an endless indulgence in jelly donuts, something cops are jokingly known for. When pressed about the reason for this career choice, I simply retorted that I wanted to arrest *you* when I got older! Maybe Mom was shocked, or maybe she was amused. But every time someone would come over to our house, she would tell me to repeat my career path to them and the reason why.

"Guess what she wants to be when she grows up?" Mom would say. "Go ahead. Tell them!"

"I want to be a cop when I grow up so I can arrest Deborah!"

How does it make you feel to know your daughter wanted to work in law enforcement just to arrest you?

Flour Game

Do you know what other childhood memories I have of you? One night, you were at our house. After you showered and put on a change of fresh clothes, you were getting ready to depart again. But, before you left, you were in the kitchen messing around with some of Mom's baking products. And since I don't ever remember you cooking a day in your life, this seemed unusual to me.

I observed you with a canister of flour, Saran Wrap, scissors and other substances. You were mixing these products together like an experienced chemist and putting the powdery mix in the plastic that you cut into round shapes. When my curiosity got to me and I

Childhood Memories

inquired of your actions, you told me it was a game. A game? Something about this curt explanation didn't sound right to me. But I did not persist.

You wrapped up your "game" in haste and headed out the door when a car horn blew. When I heard the door shut, I quickly ran to Mom's room and told her what I saw. I was considered a tattle tale in my household, but I didn't care!

Mom made a face to express her disapproval of your actions, but didn't say much beyond that. I did not know fully, at the time, what you were up to, but as an adult, I now realize you were creating a product to look like drugs with the expectation of selling it.

Your reckless action could have resulted in more than just jail time. Don't you know you could have lost your life by scheming on unsuspecting people in hopes of parting them from their money? You were right by saying it was a game. However, that was a dangerous game you were playing! You should thank God someone didn't pull out a knife and slit your throat for selling them a bogus product! Is there no end to your lies and shady practices? Is there anything that you would *not* do for money?

Drill Team

Drill teams were a popular form of recreation and exercise when I was growing up. Neighborhood girls would come together in formation, somewhat like a marching band or step team, and recite songs that corresponded with choreographed steps. It was a combination of sassy lyrics, feet stomping, hands clapping, and hips swaying. They didn't perform for anyone. There were no competitions or trophies. It was just good, old-fashion recreation and a way to enjoy being outdoors. This was a staple in urban communities.

There were a group of girls walking through the neighborhood one sunny summer day. They were going to and fro looking for as many girls as possible to recruit for a neighborhood drill team. I was walking to the corner store with you at the same time. I was really walking *behind* you, as my little legs could not keep up with your pace.

 At that moment, our path crossed with the group of drill team hopefuls. The older girl of the group, clearly the leader, approached you and asked if your daughter could join their troupe she was creating. She assumed I was your daughter simply because I was walking with you at that time, but certainly not because you had a visible presence in the neighborhood.

You offered no response. She repeated her request as though you did not hear her the first time. I looked up at you with wide eyes in anticipation of an affirmative reply. I soooo wanted to join a drill team! Drill team girls always looked cool as they performed in unison. I also figured if I teamed up with them, they wouldn't pick on me. Neighborhood kids were quick to want to call me names or want to fight. And since I didn't go to public school with most of them, I wasn't intimately acquainted with a lot of the kids in my neighborhood, nor were they with me.

You continued to walk away with your nose in the air, never making eye contact with the young lady addressing you. My hopes of joining the girls diminished, and I continued walking behind you with my head hung low, embarrassed by your action and disappointed by your inaction.

Red Sweater

Growing up, Christmas was, and still is, my favorite time of the year. In addition to celebrating Jesus' birth, there's something about the twinkling lights, gathering of loved ones, aroma of sweet potato pie, and spirit of giving to others that excite me. Mom used to have decorations everywhere: around all the inside doorways, on every window, on our white Christmas tree, and around the doorway outside.

Our tradition was to open our gifts right after midnight. Every anxious child's dream! I must say, one Christmas, you scored big on a scam or something, because you actually bought me gifts or gave Mom money to buy me gifts. I don't remember which. I wasn't allowed to open them up though at our normal midnight time frame because you specifically requested that you wanted to be present when I opened them. After all, it was *your* ill-gotten funds that subsidized Christmas that year. We waited hours for your arrival. Finally, you showed up, and I was allowed to dive into my red and green-colored boxes. This was the one and only time you bought me a Christmas gift. It was the one and only time you bought me *any* gift. Except for the red sweater.

One year, Mom received a package in the mail. It was a bright red, scoop neck, cable-knit sweater in my size. The red sweater was a Christmas gift for me from you. Apparently, there are organizations out there that send gifts to children who have parents who are incarcerated. You just provide a size and an address I suppose. You were locked up yet again, and this was your only means of sending me a gift. I suppose this is a noble idea. Organizations making sure children who don't have parents still have packages under the tree so they don't feel the absence of the invisible parents.

For me though, that red sweater was still a reminder that you were standing on the sidelines of my life, not getting involved in the game because your head was elsewhere. It was a reminder that you were still doing ungodly acts that landed you right back behind prison walls. If you were living a normal life and taking care of me, you would not have had to have some not-for-profit send me a gift on your behalf.

Childhood Memories

Physical Abuse

I was about eight years old when you got married, not that I witnessed the courthouse nuptials or anything. He was a tall, slender guy of a mixed race. I guess that was your type. The two of you acted very giddy around each other, and you appeared to be happy – for a brief moment. Out of that union came your second born. My brother David was the cutest little baby boy I had ever seen! It wasn't long though before he would be in the care of someone other than you. You were developing a pattern of maternal detachment.

Still unstable, neither you nor your new husband was in any position to care for my brother. David was also taken in by a grandmother, his father's mother. But he used to visit with us on the weekends.

One weekend, we discovered an ugly truth about your new marriage. Your husband was physically abusive, and your battle scars were highly visible. The two of you showed up to our house. You were sporting an arm sling, courtesy of your fighting husband. In addition to a broken arm, you suffered from cracked ribs.

This didn't sit well with Mom.

Mom was as tough as nails, and she was one to protect her family. She wasn't the little old grandmother knitting in her rocking chair. She was the matriarch who kept a shot gun behind her bedroom door, a pistol in her drawer and a hatchet always at her reach. Mom could keep her guns out without the fear of us touching them, because we knew better!

When Mom emerged downstairs with her shot gun in her hand, we knew something was about to go down. She unkindly let your husband know that if he continued to beat you, she would kill him. Mom chased him around the circular flow of the house – from the kitchen, through the hallway, across the living room and back through the kitchen. She yelled out threats the entire time, and he knew she wasn't playing. The pursuit eventually ended up outside on the front lawn. I'm surprised no one called the police!

While all of this was going on, I grabbed my baby brother who was about nine months old, and I ran upstairs. Sitting at the top of the stairs and still hearing all the commotion below, I cuddled him tightly and told him it would be okay because I would protect and take care of him.

No Pictures

Deborah, my childhood memories of you are quite different than the average daughter's memories of her mother. I wish I had those same positive experiences others have had, like watching television together or playing board games. But that's not my story. You robbed me of that.

Mom always kept photo albums full of family photographs and cherished memories. Someone was

Childhood Memories

always taking pictures. She also had beautifully-framed photos on all the table spaces and strategically placed on a glass étagère shelf. With all the photos everywhere, you would think there would have been at least one with the two of us in it. I have none. That's indicative of having a phantom mother. No presence + no memories = no pictures.

Charles Lisa

Chapter 7

I Wasn't Doing That When I Was Your Age!

Oftentimes, being reared in a home where there is a generation gap means there is a disconnect in how a caregiver relates to a child. Society is always evolving, but grandparents who are "stuck in their ways" do not always evolve with the times.

Mom was no exception. I loved her dearly and would not be who I am without her influence, but there are definitely some life lessons I missed out on because *you* made the choice to not be present. For instance, I never received the "sex talk."

One Sunday after church, I decided I was going to intentionally miss the bus that I would normally get on to go home and go visit a guy friend who lived around the corner from church instead. We weren't really dating, but I had a huuuuuuge crush on him! I was about 15 years old, and he was a few years older than me. He was a drummer/singer at the church I was attending. By that time, I was no longer going to a Catholic church but a Baptist one instead.

So, after church, he invited me to stop by his house where he lived with his mother and brother. We just sat there on the couch talking about nothing. As a quiet and passive child and young adult, my conversation was limited. I was just elated to be in his presence! I had him alone – all to myself – this guy that all the girls were crazy about! I was just mesmerized by his beautiful hazel-colored eyes and his perfectly manicured curly hair! So much so that I missed the *next* bus that I was supposed to get on to take me back home on the other side of town. It was a Sunday, so the 29 Wohlers bus was only running every hour. Certainly, I lost track of time, but at that point, I just decided I was going to suffer the consequences. This might have been my first act of defiance!

Of course, all of this was pre-mobile phones, so there was no way for Mom to track me. When I finally got home, I made up some story about how I kept missing the bus. She knew I was lying.

After she let this situation marinate a bit, and after she finished gossiping with one of her friends about it (I heard her on the phone,) she came into my room where I was lying in bed reading. She stood in the doorway and said, "I'm lettin you know right now, if you come home pregnant, you gettin the hell outta here! I'll kick you out on the streets!" Then she walked away. That was the extent of my sex talk…don't come home pregnant!

Mom was definitely "old school," and her generation did not talk much about sex. I believe the absence of open and honest communication between parent and child about sex and the human body is a form of fear, and in some ways ignorance, that has been passed down through generations. Unfortunately, the negligence of this parental obligation has left so many young ladies *and* young men vulnerable in this area.

I was no exception. At the age of 17, I got pregnant. Yes, I – the person with the good grades who grew up sheltered and in a strict household – fell victim to a predacious, manipulative and lying man! Although I can't blame him for my actions and choices, he was still an older guy who should have never pursued a teenage girl. He is someone who approached me on Niagara Street one day while I was walking home from my summer youth job. At 16 years old, I enjoyed the attention, I suppose. Because he lied to me, I didn't know his true age – seven years older than me - until much later. I became the negative statistic I never wanted to be. Going through this experience was probably the most trying, confusing and uncertain time of my life. The time I needed you the most, you were not there to prevent nor alleviate the situation at hand. Your guidance was non-existent.

This was not supposed to happen to *me*. This happened to my first cousins who got pregnant in their early teens. This happened to my classmates who were having babies in high school at alarming rates. But, this was not supposed to happen to me who was on an academic trajectory to catapult me into a world of business and entrepreneurship.

But the reality is that the State of New York, and the United States as a whole, were at the height of the teenage pregnancy epidemic in 1992, the same year I gave birth. That year, there were 960,000 teenage pregnancies in this country, one of the highest rates since 1980! Seventy-thousand were right in New York. It seemed like they were all at McKinley High School with me!

When I was pregnant, Papa's health was steadily failing, and he finally succumbed to complications from diabetes when I was in my eighth month of pregnancy. When the news of his death reached you all the way in North Carolina where you were staying at the time, you got on the Greyhound – with two small children in tow – and made your way to Buffalo to be with your family during this sorrowful time. Although you missed the actual funeral, you made it to town the next day nonetheless.

When you arrived at our house, two shocking revelations occurred. One, we were all shocked to find out you had *another* baby who was just four months old. And two, you were shocked when you saw me and realized I was eight months pregnant.

The first thing that came out of your mouth when you saw me was, "I wasn't doing that when I was your age!" Not, "Hello." "How are you?" "Sorry that you just lost your grandfather." No. Your words were judgmental and condemning. You tried to cut me down with your

I Wasn't Doing That When I Was Your Age!

tongue as you've done many times in the past. And really Deborah, can you truly be shocked or disappointed by my pregnancy? It's not like you can say, "I didn't raise you this way!" I can understand why Mom was disappointed. Heck, I was disappointed in myself. But you had no right sounding off at me the way you did.

Feeling like your words were sharp and unnecessary, do you remember who came to my rescue and fired back at your remarks? MOM! I didn't expect that from her since she was not pleased with the fact I was pregnant in the first place. But she said to you, "Oh, leave that girl alone. You were doing everything else when you were her age!" Ha! She shut you up with her response!

I was 17, nearing the end of my pregnancy, in my senior year of high school, working long hours at Burger King where I was standing on my feet all day and mourning the loss of my grandfather.

After work one day, I just wanted to come home, wash the French fry stench off me, then get in bed. I tried to lie down, but I was disrupted by my cousin Jackie who came in my room and shut the door behind her. She handed me a paper towel with a piece of jewelry inside of it. She told me she found it underneath the pillow in the room where you were sleeping. See, everyone knew of your reputation, and my cousin knew to do an inventory check since you were getting ready to return to North Carolina the next day. After all, she had been a victim of your self-centered ways in the past.

The two of you used to argue whenever you were around. You were always borrowing or using her items without asking permission, as if you were entitled to everyone else's belongings. Well, I did not appreciate your "help yourself mentality".

I was enraged when I found out that the piece of jewelry wrapped up in that paper towel was an emerald and diamond ring I purchased a few years earlier. You stole my emerald ring that I had stored away "safely" in my black musical jewelry box!

Well, when I found out, I immediately wanted to confront you about this. When I demanded to know why you stole my ring, you were screaming at me as if *I* was in the wrong! Then, you lunged at me and grabbed me. My cousin had to get in between us. It was wrong for you to want to fight your pregnant daughter, or anyone who is pregnant for that matter! What if I would have lost my baby? Or, what if she was harmed because of your violence? You didn't care. I think you were more upset about getting caught stealing and not being able to profit from your crime.

I was glad to see you leave. Good riddance. You were so nasty on the outside – meaning, when you're not in jail. You took whatever you wanted from whomever you wanted to take from, and you did it with an attitude as

I Wasn't Doing That When I Was Your Age!

if you were entitled. It was a different story though whenever you were locked up. You would pretend to be nice in all those sappy letters you penned from jail, and each letter started or ended with an ask.

Just five months after "Ring-gate," you were right back at your second home – jail. You wrote me on August 7, 1992, from behind bars. This was your first communication since you tried to jump on me while I was pregnant, but you began the letter as if nothing happened. You talked about wanting to know what my daughter's full name was. Perhaps you ran out of aliases and wanted to steal her identity next! You wanted to know what college I was going to and how you hated that I was no longer interested in modeling. I know, irresponsible of me to want to go to college instead of trying to become a model! And you talked about how my father was supposed to send you pictures and a copy of the program from my high school graduation. How dare he not give in to your jailhouse demands?

Then, somewhere at the very bottom of the page, you offered some sort of half-hearted apology for your actions that occurred five months earlier.

> *"I'm sorry about what I did when I was home. I just wanted to take something to remember you by."*

You wanted to take something to remember me by? What kind of lousy apology is that? You were trying to justify your actions and insult my intelligence at the same time! You were not trying to take my ring for sentimental value. You were looking for something with monetary value to take to the pawn shop and get money for it. See Deborah, that is why your words were unbelievable to me.

Mom used to always say, "I can't stand a liar and a thief!" Turns out you were both.

Charles Lisa

Chapter 8

Once a Thief, Always a Thief

After college and reaching such a momentous milestone in my life, I found myself looking for something else meaningful to get involved in. That's when I began navigating the world of politics. Through some connections I made while interning with the Buffalo Convention and Visitor's Bureau, I joined a political and civic organization making a difference in inner city Buffalo.

I was a novice when it came to politics. I managed to vote every year since my 18th birthday, but that was the extent of my involvement and understanding until I found Grassroots. This was a welcoming environment where people of all ages came together to tackle issues most prevalent in our communities. Founded by a small group of ambitious, mostly 30 something year olds, Grassroots has a *take over the world, it takes a village, neighborhood pride, respect our voice, strength in numbers, force to be reckoned with* type of atmosphere. And I loved it!

The "giving back" aspect of the organization really lured me. I felt an obligation to assist in the park clean ups, bone marrow drives and food basket giveaways. My then five-year-old daughter, "Ride or Die Dominique," was by my side the whole time, picking up debris in the parks with gloved hands like everyone else and riding along in the back seat of the car as I delivered food during the holidays to needy families.

My dedication to Grassroots got the attention of the president, who had his own trusted inner circle of young members in the organization who he was grooming. He loved to surround himself by smart, talented, young people who had a lot to offer, but who were still coachable. Once he discovered my professional talents, I quickly became part of that inner circle.

With a degree in communication, I became the go-to person for all the communication needs of the organization. I spent many late nights designing political literature and newspaper ads, writing radio scripts, sending out news releases, writing newspaper articles, editing video, and creating PowerPoint presentations and anything else the president called on me to do.

With all these new responsibilities, I needed a laptop so I could spend less time at headquarters toiling on the desktop until the wee hours of the morning and more time working in the comfort of my own home. And besides, Dominique was still right by my side most nights, and it wasn't appropriate to keep her out all night while I worked. It became a running joke at headquarters when she would put two folding chairs together, grab someone's coat, cover herself up and lay down for a nap when she was exhausted after our long days.

Seeing my need, the organization purchased a laptop for me to take home and work at my leisure. So, in between getting signatures on petitions, doing "lit drops," handing out political literature at polling sites on Primary and Election Day, I also went home to do more work. Politics quickly became my life.

After spending time in North Carolina, Deborah, you were back living in Buffalo around this time, surrounded by the same streets that sucked you into a life of crime. Mom was, of course, taking care of your two young daughters you left in her care. Unlike when she was rearing me, she was now living in a two-family home she bought, so she had plenty of room for my siblings, my cousin who she was also rearing, and anyone else who needed a place to stay. Seems like people were always coming and going when they needed transitional housing. I was no longer living with Mom at that time but was her tenant in the three-bedroom apartment upstairs.

You dropped by one day unexpected and unannounced as usual, and I wish I could say you came to check on your children or even your grandchild. I figured you were just looking for a quiet moment to plan your next move.

But, something was different. You demonstrated signs of motivation. An eagerness to get your life on track. There was hope in your voice. You talked about being a changed person and wanting to do the right thing for your children. I didn't know who this Deborah was, but I was happy to meet her!

In the many letters you've penned from prison over the years, you always talked a good game, but your words just weren't believable because they were redundant and filled with empty promises and disappointment. They were crafted for sympathy to convince us to send you money for your prison commissary account.

Hearing you speak positively was encouraging. "Could this be my answered prayers?" I thought.

The first thing you wanted to do was obtain your birth certificate from City Hall so you could apply for a driver's license or some form of identification. I was more than happy to offer you the $10 needed to get a copy.

You were trying to put things in place to get ready for a job interview you told me about. You talked about the secretarial skills you learned and certificates you earned while locked up. So, when you asked me if you could borrow my laptop to brush up on your typing skills in preparation for your job interview, I was more than eager to assist!

This was the proudest I had ever been of you.

Once a Thief, Always a Thief

I went upstairs to my apartment to retrieve my laptop and brought it downstairs to you. You were grateful for the opportunity I had given you.

I was only back upstairs in my apartment for a hot minute when I heard the sound of the exit door slam. By the time I ran to the window, your getaway car sped off and was no longer in sight. You, along with Grassroots' laptop, were gone. I never saw it again.

My short-lived proud moment of you, Deborah, turned into a nightmare. Your talk of change and betterment was nothing more than a ruse to steal.

I was angry at your deceit. I felt let down by your false hope. But mostly, I was embarrassed because I had to go before the leadership of Grassroots to explain how my mother stole the laptop purchased by the organization.

Until that occurrence, I hadn't clued them in on my family dysfunction. But I was forced to expose the ugliness that I had to endure in my life. I was the beloved "little sister" of the group held in high regard. I was a dedicated member in good standing.

Fearing my image and reputation would be tainted by *your* actions, I put on my big girl pants anyway and told the president what had occurred, regardless of any repercussions I feared would follow. The reaction wasn't as bad as I thought it would be. After several exclamations of, "Your mother did what?" he bought me another laptop, but this time, I had to pay for half of it.

Deborah, imagine how successful you would be if you used that same passion for crime in a legitimate way. You have a persistence, perseverance and drive that would outshine any business tycoon. What if you harness that energy into positive productivity? Education? A job? A cause? Making amends with those you have hurt?

HAZEL B LITTLE — ORDER OF SERVICE — FAMILY TREE

IN GOD'S CARE NOW

Hazel B. Little

Sunrise
April 12, 1920

Sunset
October 23, 1998

Wednesday October 28, 1998 - 11:00 a.m.
Funeral: noon

Jerusalem Baptist Church
465 Glenwood Avenue
Buffalo, New York 14211
Rev. Precious L. Thompson Pastor
Officiating

"To God Be The Glory"

Chapter 9

The Hole in the Ceiling

After a month of lying in a hospital bed, Mom finally got a diagnosis. "I have CN," she whispered to me one night when I went to visit her at Erie County Medical Center. "CN? What's that?" I asked. She whispered and spoke in code because my daughter and my youngest sister were with me, and she didn't want to alarm the children. Not that they would have known what she was talking about anyway.

"I have cancer," she said staring into space calmly yet with a tone indicating the finale of her life. For a split second, my heart stopped. My body was frozen. A slew of thoughts ran through my mind instantly. However, they were quickly interrupted by her next words. "But I'm not worried because I'm going home to live with Jesus."

Then, I was overtaken by a sense of peace. I believe it was the peace that the Bible speaks of:

> *"And the peace of God, which surpasses all understanding, will guard your hearts and minds through Christ Jesus."*
> - Philippians 4:7 NKJV

And I needed that peace in order to absorb, comprehend and execute the instructions that followed. She proceeded to tell me what to do with her house, jewelry, furs, expensive clothes and televisions. She gave me specific orders on where she wanted to be buried. "Make sure you take my body back home," she instructed. "Back home" is in Louisiana where we have a host of relatives buried at a cemetery about a mile away from the dirt road where Mom grew up. Your sister Barbara, grandparents, uncles and a cousin are all buried there.

Mom asked me not to tell anyone of her fate yet. I suppose she wanted to tell it in her own way, on her own time. But her time was finite, quickly coming to an end.

There was nothing more the hospital could do for her. So, after a few days, and I imagine after coercing from hospital staff who wanted to turn over her bed for the next patient they could make money off of, Mom decided it was time to tell the rest of the family. She told me to gather the family at the hospital so she could tell everyone at once. But Mom was very explicit about who she did *not* want at the hospital. "WHATEVER YOU DO, DON'T TELL DEBORAH! I DON'T WANT HER AROUND. SHE JUST GONNA RAISE ALL KINDS OF HELL! AND I DON'T WANT HER FIGHTING OVER MY STUFF!" Mom exclaimed.

The Hole in the Ceiling

How does it feel to know that your own mother, on her death bed, didn't even want to lay eyes on you? Didn't want you in her presence? Didn't want to share her final moments with you, the last child she birthed?

I certainly can't speak for the dead, but perhaps, she remembered the moments she *did* share with you. I imagine at the time she played a tape in her head of all the times you stole from her. Maybe, she recalled all the disappointments, jail visits, heartaches and sleepless nights worrying about you. I would guess she thought about all the drug-induced rage you displayed. Or, maybe she laid there pondering where she went wrong with you.

It's not like I knew where to find you to tell you Mom was sick. I never knew where you laid your head at night. I hadn't heard from you, which means you were out in the streets and not in jail. And besides, I didn't want to hear from you anyway. Just months earlier, you stole my laptop!

I could definitely understand why she didn't want you to know she was dying of cancer. Nothing good *ever* came about when you were around.

Two weeks after Mom's diagnosis, she died. October 23, 1998, was the saddest day of my life. I had just gotten off work and went down the street to Aunt Earlene's house to pick up my daughter and sister so I could make it back to the hospital. But there was no need to after I got a phone call delivering news of the inevitable.

Mom's death caused a shift in the atmosphere. When I looked to my right and to my left, I came to a sobering conclusion. I was an orphan. By definition, an orphan is a child who has lost both parents through death. Ironically, both of my parents were still alive. Yet, I was still an orphan. The only person that played a parental role in my life had passed. I had never felt more alone. Mom was the nucleus of the family. She was my support system.

But I had to hold it all together and get through the arrangements. When I made it home after picking up the girls, the doorbell rang. I opened the window facing the driveway to see who it was. "OPEN THE DOOR!" you yelled in a surly voice. Even in the face of adversity and bereavement, Deborah, you couldn't be nice.

I went downstairs to open the door, and as soon as you stepped in the hallway, you broke down and cried. That was the first time I ever saw you cry. In between sobs, you blurted out expressions like, "Why didn't anybody tell me she was sick?" and, "My Momma went to hell because she wasn't saved!" Went to hell? Not saved? Deborah, you clearly didn't know your own mother!

You quickly made yourself comfortable in her home. Thankfully, I had already confiscated the items Mom instructed me to take care of. Or else, they would have walked away just like the other items you helped yourself to.

Mom's funeral was five days after her death. Within that week, I designed her obituary, made arrangements for her friend and pastor Reverend Thompson to eulogize her, received an out-of-town guest, and completed other items that needed to be taken care of. But the one task I participated in that was especially endearing was going to the funeral home with other family members where we assisted in preparing the body. I never thought I would be in a room filled with dead bodies and be at peace! But there we were, putting on her wig and makeup and laughing about how the funeral director polished her nails halfway as if it was some French manicure! The funeral director, who was familiar with Mom, was used to seeing her with her nails that way, so he thought it was intentional. What he didn't realize was she often needed to go to the nail salon for a "fill" because her nails grew rapidly, thus looking like half of her nail was polished. We all agreed that a simple lace glove would be appropriate to cover up the bad nail polish job that we did not have time to fix.

The day of Mom's funeral was the first and last time you, my siblings and I had ever been in the same room together. It was the only time we "looked like" a family.

After songs were sung, expressions of love were spoken and a eulogy was delivered, we gathered around the coffin one last moment at the end before it was time for the funeral home to take the coffin away in preparation for her body to be flown to Louisiana. This was the first time I cried over Mom's death. I think my tears were caused by the sight of my cousins crying. I had not shed a tear up until that moment. Too busy trying to take care of business. But I certainly have dropped plenty of tears since. Over 19 years later, I still tear up out of the blue with thoughts of her. It doesn't matter if I'm at home, at work, or at the doctor's office as I am right now with watery eyes.

Sometimes, I cry when I'm remembering her teachings. Or, I cry when I think about how she didn't get a chance to witness my spiritual growth. Other times, I'm wishing she could have experienced the comforts of life I could have provided to her if she was still around. Or, I'm simply rejoicing over the sacrifices she made for me, like taking care of my baby every day while I was attending Buffalo State College or at work.

Do you think you have positively impacted anyone's life? Would anyone cry for you, Deborah, when you're gone?

The day after Mom's funeral, my cousin and I drove to Louisiana. Twenty-four hours later, we made our way down that narrow, dirt road in Wilson where Mom's brother lives in a trailer on the land where they grew up. It was the same place I used to love visiting every summer as a child. My uncle has greens and other

The Hole in the Ceiling

edibles growing on his property, sassafras trees which make great tea, deer running around as if they own the place, and fruit trees lining the back of his property line. He had the same "grow your own" mindset that my grandmother had, and he is quite content "living off the land in God's country," as he would say.

A small group of family members gathered at the funeral home in Louisiana. My uncle, who is normally jovial, playing practical jokes on people or making everyone laugh, had the most solemn face I had ever seen him express. When he approached the white coffin to view Mom's body, he said to me, "Your grandmother sure was a beautiful woman."

It was a short and sweet memorial. Immediately afterwards, everyone drove to St. Paul's Cemetery where Mom requested to be buried. The vault that holds her spiritless body lay beside one of her brothers. After a brief prayer, we said our final goodbyes as her body was lowered into the ground. I was able to fulfill her dying wish.

Before I left Buffalo to travel to Louisiana, I asked a friend to stay at my house while I was away. I requested her presence simply to look after the house because with you around, something was bound to happen. It was a necessary precaution; however, Mom's coats and jewelry were safely stored down the street at my aunt's house, and her expensive clothes were with me in

Louisiana because she instructed me to give them to one of her nieces there.

I checked in with my friend constantly while I was away, and she assured me that everything was fine back at the house.

Unfortunately, when I got back to Buffalo, everything was *not* fine. When I arrived home, I found my front door hanging off the hinges. It wasn't the outside door, but the door leading upstairs to my apartment after entering the shared hallway.

Somehow, you managed to take the screws out of the hinges, and you removed the door. Whether you had an accomplice or not, I do not know. But I *do* know that you will go to great lengths to destroy anything that gets in the way of you ripping off your next victim.

Infiltrating through my front door wasn't your first choice of breaking and entering. Downstairs in Mom's house was evidence of your other failed scheme to break into my house and pilfer whatever you thought was of value. With Mom's famed hatchet, you devised a plan to bust through the ceiling in her bathroom and tunnel your way upstairs. Who does that? Deborah, that's who! I don't know if someone walked in on your crime, or whether your arm got tired from standing on a chair swinging that hatchet, but for some reason you didn't finish the task. The only feat you accomplished was putting a big hole in the bathroom ceiling.

The Hole in the Ceiling

Mom was so wise. The older I get, the more I realize how wise she was. She discerned that something like this would happen. It's evident in her pre-death command to not alert you of her deteriorating health.

Deborah, what was going through your mind at that time as you were standing on a chair with a hatchet, attempting to penetrate layers of sheetrock and ceiling joists? Or when you were prying the screws out of the door hinges? This was a time of grief, but instead, you turned it into a time of greed.

After learning of all this commotion that occurred while I was in Louisiana, I asked my house sitter why she didn't tell me on the phone when I was checking in with her daily. She simply said she didn't want me to worry about what was going on in Buffalo while I was away burying my grandmother. She made a good choice. I would have been fuming the entire drive home had I known what you were up to.

The phone calls continued to come in as concerned people checked up on me, as they knew how great my loss was. I received one such call from my former boss who was the Masten District councilman at the time. After all I had been through, it was so refreshing to get that call. But, I was still wounded from your actions, and I couldn't help but to tell him about the hole in the ceiling and the door hanging off the hinges. He was shocked that someone could do this sort of heinous act, especially at a time such as it was. Initially, I was ashamed to tell an elected official – or anyone for that matter – that I had a mother who would carry on like that. But, then I concluded that I would not be clothed in your shame anymore, and there was no need to keep silent.

With Mom gone, my little sister naturally moved upstairs with me. My other sister was already in a foster home before Mom passed. Being a 24-year-old single mother at that time, I was not prepared financially or emotionally to care for another child. My sister was the same age as my daughter, and they kept each other company, but this was an unexpected turn of events.

Before I could begin to figure out how I was going to take on this challenge, a cousin stepped up and asked me if she could take my sister into her custody. She expressed an interest in not only adopting her, but getting my other sister out of foster care and adopting her as well. My cousin has a son, but always wanted a little girl. This seemed like the perfect solution to my dilemma. I was relieved.

My sister immediately transitioned into my cousin's care as soon as we agreed on that arrangement. The only thing that was left to do was make it legal through family court. My cousin wanted me to accompany her to court because, after all, someone credible had to bear witness to how my sister went to live with a relative. Or else, the judge might have thought she was kidnapped or something! So, I obliged.

The Hole in the Ceiling

Our day in court came a few months after Mom passed, and there you were, sitting there in handcuffs. I didn't expect you to even be there, let alone be confined in handcuffs. Surprise, surprise! You were arrested yet again, for what only God knows. I guess that's how the court could serve you papers to show up in family court because you were already in custody.

When the judge finally posed his questions to me, I simply explained to him how my sister was in our grandmother's care before she passed. I also had a hand-written letter signed by you, Deborah, years earlier stating that you could not care for your children, and you were leaving them with your mother.

You somehow devised a plan for a woman you knew to take my sister instead. As if you even had a say in the matter! For whatever reason, you would have rather she stayed with this random person than a family member. You even had her appear in court that day. Unfortunately, you wasted that woman's time, because the judge did not take your request into consideration. You were so infuriated with *me*, that you left out of the court room screaming at me and yelling all sorts of profanity. As the sheriff dragged you out of there, you had the audacity to call me the "B word"!

I don't think anyone had ever used that word to describe me with such hatred. I was confused. What did I do to deserve such venom that spewed out of your mouth? You were seriously mad at me, Deborah, because I went to court to ensure the safety and welfare of my sister?

Clearly you were. In a letter you wrote to my father from jail on December 11, 1998, you told him exactly how you felt about me.

"Your daughter and I are through FOR LIFE. She's a turn coat... Charles Lisa has absolutely no respect for me, and she accompanied this girl to family court on 12-7 against me so the girl could get custody of my 6 yr. old. She didn't respect the fact that I have someone of my own choice to come to court... I could go on and on about her rotten a__ but I won't cause you will only defend her instead of teaching her to have respect for her mother. I have no intentions of speaking to her for the rest of my life."

The rest of your life or the next time you want something? Either you forgot your harsh words you spoke against me to my father or you didn't intend for me to read that letter, but four months later, you were writing me and begging for me to fulfill your "send me this, send me that" wish list as usual. You started off the letter by saying:

"Is there any chance in you 'ever' doing anything I ask you to do?"

How could you address me like that, then turn around and make a request of me? Was that line supposed to motivate me to want to do something for you? Better

The Hole in the Ceiling

yet, how could you even have the audacity to ask me for *anything* after your courthouse scene, name calling and subsequent backbiting in your letter to my father? Not to mention all the other atrocities in the past.

Your letter was cold. It lacked warmth and read as if nothing happened four months prior. Deborah, this has always been your mode of operation. You have chosen to harm me over and over through your words and actions, then you would act as if nothing ever happened. And I was supposed to magically erase all your actions from my memory.

You have always treated me as if I owed you something. Me. The daughter who *you* neglected. Then, when I wouldn't cave in to your demands, you would look upon me with such disdain.

I don't deserve your hatred. Your disrespect. Your animosity. Your vile behavior. I deserve love. Concern. Tenderness. Support. I deserve a mother.

Charles Lisa

Chapter 10

The Letters

One thing you were consistent at was writing letters whenever you were in jail. It seems like I've been reading your letters ever since I was old enough to read. You have a pretty neat penmanship, but I guess that came with plenty of practice!

When I was a child, all your letters were addressed to me. But even so, Mom read them first before I even saw them. One time, I observed her steam opening an envelope using the hot water from her daily morning coffee. After she read it, she sealed it back up and then gave it to me. I never revealed to her that I knew what she was doing. I don't know if she was just being nosey or if she just wanted to shield me from whatever lies or hurt she thought would appear in your letters. Mom was always trying to protect me.

You spelled my name several different ways on the envelope whenever you would write. Deborah, do you not know how to spell your own daughter's name? I mean, you named me for goodness sakes! Between your misspellings and Mom's phonetic spelling, it's no wonder why I didn't learn how to spell my name correctly until I was 14 years old. When I applied for the Mayor's Summer Youth Employment Program, I saw my birth certificate for the first time. My eyes widened as I looked at all the extra consonants and vowels I never knew belonged there. I have been telling people for years to just call me Lisa because of all the confusion surrounding my name. It certainly isn't spelled the way it's pronounced. I don't know why parents do this to their children's names!

The Begging

I didn't begin saving your letters until high school. Do you know that I have every letter you have written me since? I bet you never expected that. In 1989 alone, you wrote five. I read back over them recently. Your words reeked with selfishness. Each letter was all about a request. What I, and others, could do for you. And a sob story that went along with your request to compel us to act.

Thursday, April 21, 1989

"I got your letter and the $50.00. Thank you very much, and thanks for writing. I was beginning to worry because I wrote you so long ago and you never wrote back…. Hurry and get a picture made."

Thursday, July 13, 1989

"Thanks a lot for the pictures. It took me this long to write to let you all know I got them because I didn't have money to buy stamps, but somebody gave me one… Since I've been here I've been wearing the same

jail clothes day after day, cause I don't have anything here. I only have 2 pr of pants, & I've been wearing the same 2 since November of 1988. When I leave here I don't want to come home to the halfway house in jail pants, and have to go for job interviews like that. There all worn out anyway. Call my sister for me and tell her I need my jacket (with the tails). I don't have nothing to walk out of here. These people don't give you nothing but bus fare, and it will be cold when I leave here… I'm going to ask Mom to buy me an outfit to wear home… I'm glad I get mail from you. People always talking behind my back, about I must don't have no family, or if so they must don't care cause I never get mail or money like them. I get wind of the gossip."

Wednesday, August 16, 1989

"I've been looking for you to write back ever since I sent you that last letter. Did my sister ever bring my jacket over (with the raccoon tails on it?) Let me know something cause once she brings it I need to ask Mom to send it to me with some other things when I get ready to go, cause it will be cold… Are you going to modeling school? If so haven't you all taken any pictures for a portfolio? I'm waiting on more pictures… Did my niece send me some shoes yet?"

Sunday, October 15, 1989

"I thought you would have written me back by now. Hasn't it been at least 2 months since I sent you the *picture of your little sister? Did you ask Mom to get a copy made for you yet? Well when you do, hurry and send me one back because that's all I have right now... You never told me whether or not you told my sister I said I need my jacket... P.S. How is my niece doing? Has she gotten me any shoes from them different countries yet?"*

Sunday, December 10, 1989

"I'm not feeling too good (sore throat and a fever) so I'm not writing much. I just wanted to know why you have not sent me something from your portfolio. If you need them all just send me 1 or 2 and I'll put them right back in the mail the same week and send them back to you. I told a lot of people I was expecting it so don't let me down okay... C if my sweet sister will send me some traveling money for Xmas. I'll save it to travel with in January. Long ride from here."

Why was I, at 14 years old, sending *you* money? Was it my job to support *you* or was it *your* job to support *me*?

You wanted everything done for you with urgency. I needed to be on *your* timetable. If I didn't write you back in a week, you were writing me another letter asking why I didn't write back yet. Well, you were locked up. You had nothing but time. I, on the other hand, had a full life I was living and didn't spend every awakening moment thinking about writing letters.

The Letters

Why was it so important for you to have pictures of me while locked up, but when you were out, I didn't see you much? Oh, I know. You told me in your letters. You wanted to show them off to your cellmates. And, I needed to send you pictures quickly to not disappoint you. You were concerned about *me* disappointing *you* and *me* failing to meet *your* expectations but you never met any of my expectations. Did you ever think about my disappointments, Deborah?

And why on earth did you feel like you needed fine Italian shoes and fur coats in prison? You were confined in a cell! You weren't going to a ball! Heck, you weren't even going to the grocery store! All you needed was exactly what "those people" gave you.

You begged for money constantly. You had this sense of entitlement as if everyone owed you something. And even though most of your letters started off with, "How are you doing," your words felt hollow to me. I couldn't feel your love or care because you made every letter about you. Did you *really* care how I was doing?

If you cared about how I was, perhaps, you should have asked me how I was feeling. How I felt about your absence. How I was handling that emptiness. If it affected me in school.

Instead of simply asking me how was school, it would have been nice if you would have talked to me about my strengths in school and helped me decide on a career path. Rather, you just obsessed over me modeling. I guess it reminded you of the narcissistic, vanity-driven, fast-money profession you chose.

In an undated letter, you wrote,

"Guess what, ever since you were a little girl I always wanted you to be a model. You must be reading my mind. That makes me very happy. Work hard at it. It takes a lot of work. A girl I went to school with is one of America's top black models, her name is Beverly Johnson. We went to school #74 together, and Bennett High School. She started out in high school too."

I'm thankful for one of my English teachers at McKinley High School who pulled me aside one day after grading one of my papers and praised me for doing a great job writing. He encouraged me to pursue a viable career where I can use my skills, rather than a career in modeling. I eventually choose a career in communications, partly because of him. Even though you "always wanted me to be a model" and "it makes you very happy," I have a feeling that you wanted to live out your own fantasies of modeling and stardom through me.

I've always loved and admired Beverly Johnson, Iman and Tyra Banks, but let's face it, these women are 5'9" and 5'10" tall. At 5'3", I would have never made it as a runway model!

The Letters

This obsession over what others needed to do for you was a pattern in *all* your letters, not just the small sampling from 1989.

Sunday, August 5, 1990

"Listen do this 2-day, ask Mom for my uncle's phone number and put it in the mail to me 2 day okay cause I need it cause I can't get nobody to bring me 5 or $10.00 so I can buy soap & stuff...Next time you go by your father's house, get some $$ from him for me."

You always wanted me to send you phone numbers and addresses for every family member you could think of. Your sole purpose was to beg for money. You really didn't care about how anyone was doing. These are the same people you mistreated or ignored when you weren't locked up. Did you really think they would be enthusiastic to get a letter from you, accept a collect call, or send you money?

You also used to write me and tell me to take the block off my phone. The only reason I had a block against collect calls on my phone was because of you! Why would you expect me to bear the expense of your collect calls, especially when you just wanted to call to beg for money?

August 1990

"I was hoping you would have written me before I left from Down Town, what happened? I never did receive

any money from your father either. Well what can I say. Maybe somebody will send me something someday. So you're going back to school next month. Hey aren't you working now? I can't tell, smile."

You can't tell? Really? I was a sophomore in high school working a summer job! You expected me to send all my minimum wage earnings to you? This from a woman who has NEVER given me any money! Well... there was that one time when I was about 19 years old. You gave me $200 of ill-gotten money, and the next day, you came back to get it because "you needed it".

December 2, 1994

"Call your father and ask him if he will buy me a carton of Newport Kings and 10.00 for Xmas. If he says yes, ask him when can you come get it. Don't let him say he will send it because I will never get it. Tell him you will send it along with everybody else's okay. But you send it to me today okay...P.S. tell my niece I want for Xmas $10.00 and you send me – socks white, green, a cake, cookies and candy TODAY."

The Stranger

As if you didn't bombard me with enough jail letters, I suddenly started receiving letters in 1994 from an acquaintance of yours who was locked up in Elmira, New York. This creepy guy that you apparently had some long distance, prison romance with started reaching out to "introduce himself to me." He started telling me about how he lusted after women's physical appearance when he was home; "their pretty face, or butt and other body parts." Then he told me how he would be "distracted at home with allowing his lower desires (SEX) to dictate" for him, rather than getting to know someone's mind as he was doing with you since he has never seen you. Why did he feel the need to talk to a young lady, your daughter, like this? The conversation was weird and very inappropriate.

I was even more disturbed when he told me you sent him pictures of me and my daughter! This strange man who was in prison, without the satisfaction of laying eyes on a woman in person, had some type of relationship with you but had never seen you, had all kinds of pictures of me so he knows exactly what I look like and expressed to me how he enjoyed women's body parts. This man was sending me letters!

He may have been "getting to know you mentally" as he expressed, but who do you think he was staring at and fantasizing about when he laid his head down at night? I felt violated that you were shipping my pictures to prisoners so you could "show me off" to strange men!

This explains the real reason why you kept begging me constantly to send you pictures of myself. Every letter you wrote, you asked for more pictures. You must have thought I was standing around all day doing nothing but photo shoots!

Not only was this strange man telling me about all the pictures he had of me, but he took up much real estate on the neatly typed pages trying to convince me he was a good guy who made a mistake, he was not a bum and I shouldn't judge him. I don't know why he was trying so hard to sell himself to me. I wanted nothing to do with this man! But there he was, writing me as if we were old friends.

On top of that, he wanted to preach to me about how you needed my support and that I needed to write you more. "Oh great!" I thought. Another letter about you and *your* needs! This passage below is an excerpt from one of his letters:

Monday, October 3, 1994

"What I am trying to do in a short time and short letter, is appeal to you to sacrifice some time and write her. I know how busy you are, because I once worked full time as well as went to college at night. You have the added task of being a mother along with that. So I can really imagine how busy you are. But know matter what, Deborah is your mother and your only one and she need you now. You might can say well you needed her and she wasn't there, well then I am certain you don't want to be guilty of the same."

His words mirrored yours when, at times, you would try to guilt me into forgiving you for your offenses against me. I'm not sure by what authority he felt he could compel me to do *anything,* but I did not solicit his advice, nor did I want it. So, next time please don't have your prison pen pals reaching out to me, Deborah!

Empty Promises

I think it's common for people to sit back and dream about future goals. I do it all the time. As a matter of fact, I have always had lofty goals. But I push, persevere and persist, so my goals are attainable, even if they seem far-fetched to others. My dreams directly affect me, so if anyone is going to be let down by failure, it's me.

You, on the other hand, sit back and dream up dreams that affect others. You have failed everyone around you with your false dreams and empty promises, including my siblings.

Thursday, July 13, 1989

"Call your brother & talk to him. I plan to go into court & get him once I'm out & get a good job, & get a lawyer, cause them people lied in the first place to get him."

August 1990

"I missed reporting to my probation officer a couple of times, and that's why she had me locked back up. But now I'm getting the sentence all over with. And I'll be free when I get out. No parole no probation. And I won't be locked up anymore okay... When I get out the first of

the year I'm going straight to North Carolina and SNEAK your sister away from her father... I've got to stay out of trouble B-4- I can get Little Dave back cause I've got to go to court."

March 8, 1990

"Don't build your hopes up just yet, but I might be coming into quite a bit of money within the next 12 months. I am about to file a BIG lawsuit, and I may become a millionaire if I win. Then I can buy Mom a house or condo, and I can buy you a car. Your too young for your own house hahaha... I've got a good case, and it may not take a whole year to collect. I'm asking for 10 million so I'll probably get 1 or 2. So we'll never be broke. Well let's see what happens."

Undated Letter

"The government sent me a grant that I can use if I want to go to college when I get out of this place... I want out of here, and when I do, I surely won't be getting into anymore trouble, that's for real... I've really got to straighten up, so I can go into court, and fight to get David, and your other little brother in Las Vegas and your sister in Rockingham. I've got to go straight first or I'm going to lose, because I don't have anyone to help me fight to get them."

November 8, 1992

The Letters

"I have to do some community service when I get out as a condition of my parole but soon as I'm done, we're gonna get on the Greyhound and head home. I'll be saving my paychecks so I can find a house or something soon as we get there."

Saturday, September 17, 1994

Deborah, you sent a letter to my house for my brother, because you feared he wouldn't get it if you sent it to his house where he was staying with his father's mother. You wanted me to take it back from him after he read it, instead of him keeping it. You wrote these words:

"If you just straighten up til I get there and don't tell nobody I'm coming, I promise you I am going to fight for you. When you were a baby you could not talk and say who you wanted to be with, but I've been waiting for you to get big enough to think for yourself… When I get there I will give you all lots of money and buy you nice things I promise and get us a house… I promise to give you whatever you want… I'm gonna be good so I can see you. You've gotta be good so you can see me. Is that a deal?"

It's easy to *say* what you will do. Actions are another story. You've made empty promises for years, but I suppose false hopes are better than saying, "I'm going to keep making bad choices year after year that will land me back in jail after I get out." Or, "I'm never going to support you financially or otherwise so don't expect anything from me." Or how about, "I will never fight to get any of my children back because I love the streets way too much!"

When you were promising to buy houses, cars and all kinds of gifts, you knew you had no way of doing that! And how were you going to get a job with no skill set?

And most importantly, how many times did you tell me and yourself that you weren't going to get into anymore trouble, only to repeat the pattern year after year? None of what you said in your letters came to pass. And, you certainly did not settle yourself down anywhere or go to court to get my brother back as you had promised him.

You talked a good game but never delivered. You've failed me, your other children and yourself.

Blame Game

Deborah, it's not your fault you've failed everyone around you, at least that's what you've said repeatedly in your letters. It's everyone else's fault.

It's Mom's fault that you turned to a life of crime.

It's your probation officer's fault that you were locked back up.

It's "those people's" fault why you did not rear your son David.

The Letters

It's the hospital's fault that you don't have your other son that you left in that Las Vegas hospital.

It's my fault my sisters ended up going into foster care before they were eventually adopted by a cousin.

It's my fault that you don't have a relationship with your granddaughter.

At what point do you take full responsibility for your actions, Deborah? When do you look in the mirror and say, "I made a mess of my life. I made bad choices. I knew right from wrong. I chose wrong."

Holding on to Past Hurts

Pain. Distrust. Hurt. Misplaced anger. Your letters captured all these feelings. When you weren't making a request, you were expounding on how everyone has wronged you. I can't dismiss your feelings; how you feel is how you feel. But, I do believe you have held on to excessive and unhealthy anger for far too long, as evident in your letters.

Excessive anger can cause people to be bitter. Deborah, you have caused bitterness to take root in your life, and it has manifested itself in various ugly ways. It's the bitterness that has caused you to make the choices you have made. But it is time to free yourself from bitterness and anger. The only way to this kind of freedom is forgiveness.

"Let all bitterness, wrath, anger, clamor, and evil speaking be put away from you, with all malice. And be kind to one another, tenderhearted, forgiving one another, even as God in Christ forgave you."

Ephesians 4:31-32 NKJV

Chapter 11

The Gift of Forgiveness

Deborah, I have wanted to express my feelings to you so many times in the past. I've rehearsed the words in my head over and over, but it has still been extremely difficult to begin. You've written me time after time and have only received silence in return. I had so much to say over the years, yet I said nothing. This letter is more than 18 years in the making. But I knew this would be the best form of communication, since it allows me to organize my thoughts concisely. It also allows me to get my point across uninterrupted and without the hostility that I want to avoid from a two-way, verbal conversation. History tells me that could be the unfortunate result.

I also took my time in writing you because, well, I knew you had nothing but time. When I learned in 1999 you were serving a 15-year prison sentence, I began. At the time I started writing, you were still locked up. When you were released a few years ago, it reignited my drive to finally finish this lengthy, didactic letter.

I want to talk to you about forgiveness. Forgiveness is a topic we often talk about in church, but I don't think Christians have a monopoly on the subject. I think it's an action that believers and non-believers alike can take part in. So, why am I even bringing up forgiveness at all? As I stated earlier, I believe forgiveness is the first step in freedom – freedom from judgment, anger, bitterness, depression, a hardened heart, painful memories, back-biting and finger pointing. The Bible talks about the subject of forgiveness at length, and I want to explore four key areas with you.

GOD'S FORGIVENESS

I don't exactly know how old you are, Deborah, but I think you're in your 60s. I know you were born in the month of March, but I don't even know your birthdate. What I do know is that in your 60+ years on earth, you have done a great deal of harm to yourself, to others and, more importantly, to God. Your sins are too numerous to count, but the Bible tells us that everyone sins, not just you. We *all* fall short of God's glorious standard (Romans 3:23). So, if God is the one setting the moral standard for how you should live, it is God who you offend every time you choose to do wrong.

The good news, though, is that God is a forgiving God! For all the times you have committed crimes, sold your body, broken into homes, stolen from people including your own mother and daughter, abandoned your children, spoke ill of people and threatened harm to them, God can and will forgive you! In fact, He considers it a gift! The Bible talks about this in the Book

The Gift of Forgiveness

of Romans (5:15). The writer Paul proclaims how God's grace – you know, that favor we don't deserve – and His gift of forgiveness comes through Jesus Christ. You recall, don't you, when you wrote to me from jail on July 22, 1993 and you told me you were saved? Well, that's what this Scripture is referring to. Because you believe Jesus Christ is your Savior, you can go to God and ask Him for forgiveness for your sins!

Deborah, stop and reflect for a moment on all the wrong you've done in your lifetime. I don't know the magnitude of your sins, but God knows them all. Close your eyes and let all the evil images, actions, thoughts and words rush into your mind. Now picture God wiping the slate clean like a teacher erasing a chalk board. He's erasing all the times you hurt Him, because He loves you too much to keep score. That's good news knowing you can start all over, and that should bring you unmeasurable joy! You may not have much in this world, but if you have that kind of joy, no one can take it away from you!

Jesus has the authority on earth to forgive sins (Mark 2:10). All of them (Mark 3:28) no matter how bad they seem to you and others. If He forgives you for all your wrong-doing, it really doesn't matter what anyone else thinks of you or your past. You should feel liberated in that!

So, when will God give you this wonderful gift called forgiveness? It's actually quite simple. Deborah, God is calling you to do four things:

1. Humble yourself
2. Pray
3. Seek His face
4. Turn from your wicked ways

According to 2 Chronicles 7:14, this is a recipe for creating the right atmosphere for God to forgive you.

Humble Yourself

Being humble isn't necessarily saying you're less than but that God is greater than! It's recognizing that there is a power higher than you, and you aren't the one who's in control. It's checking your arrogance at the door and leaving it there. It's realizing that you are nothing without the one who gives you life. And, It's being courteous and respectful, even if you don't agree with someone. Humility is also shedding the expectation that everyone in this world owes you something, especially without you giving anything in return, as you've done so many times in the past, Deborah.

As you know, the opposite of humility is pride. And, if the Bible tells us to humble ourselves, God must frown upon pride! In fact, He considers it to be evil, and lists it among other sins that defile or pollute a person's heart:

"For from within, out of a person's heart, come evil thoughts, sexual immorality, theft, murder, adultery, greed, wickedness, deceit, lustful desires, envy, slander, pride, and foolishness. All these vile things come from within; they are what defile you."
- Mark 7:21-23 NLT

I love the book of Proverbs, because there is no shortage of passages that speak to what happens when you let pride reign in your life, Deborah:

- *"When **pride** comes, then comes **shame**; But with the humble is wisdom." - Proverbs 11:2 NKJV*

- *"By **pride** comes nothing but **strife**, But with the well-advised is wisdom." - Proverbs 13:10 NKJV*

- ***"Pride** goes before **destruction**, And a haughty spirit before a fall." – Proverbs 16:18 NKJV*

Have you ever experienced shame, strife or destruction in your life? Perhaps, you can attribute that to your pride! Just remember, pride will bring you low, but if you have a humble spirit, you will retain honor (Proverbs 29:23)!

Pray

Prayer is simply having a conversation with God. We don't have to use fancy language or try to impress Him with complicated sentences. There are plenty of people who have no problems communicating with friends, family members and co-workers every day. Even the most socially-awkward individuals will take to social media and blogs to pen messages to strangers on a regular basis as a form of communication. But, for some reason, it's difficult to have constant communication with God. I don't know if you are in that category, Deborah, but I know I am sometimes, and a whole lot of other Christians if they are honest with themselves! Even with all the wonderful things I know about Him, with all the miracles I've witnessed and all the grace I've received, it still can be difficult. But it shouldn't be. After all, God already knows what's in our hearts and on our minds! And Jesus has even given us a model prayer to guide us for those who don't know how to pray.

> *"Our Father in heaven, hallowed be Your name. Your kingdom come. Your will be done on earth as it is in heaven. Give us this day our daily bread. And forgive us our debts, as we forgive our debtors. And do not lead us into temptation, but deliver us from the evil one. For Yours is the*

kingdom and the power and the glory forever. Amen." – Matthew 6:9-13 NKJV

So, Deborah, if you want God to forgive you, you should pray to him, tell Him what you've done and ask for forgiveness as the Scripture directs you to. It's that easy! I John 1:9 (NLT) says, "But if we confess our sins to him, he is faithful and just to forgive us our sins and to cleanse us from all wickedness." Ask Him to forgive you of all your debts; all your trespasses; all the times you've sinned against Him! Ask Him to give you strength to sin no more. Ask Him to show you how to live right. Ask Him to guide your footsteps so that He's in control instead of you. Ask Him to take away the urge to steal, do drugs, fornicate, lie, fill in the blank...

Seek His Face

Deborah, after you humble yourself and pray, you then have to seek God's will. After all, *your* will hasn't really led to great success. God rewards those who diligently seek Him (Hebrews 11:6). If you want to know what God's will is – what He requires of you and this world – go no further than the Bible. This book really is a true blueprint for how to live according to God's will. Reading the Bible will help you get to know who God is in an intimate way. It's like dating. When you meet someone you're interested in, you stay up all night talking on the phone, and when you're not talking, you're texting messages in between calls or Skyping so you can see his or her face when you're apart. You can't get enough of that person! Before you know it, you're in a relationship. You should have that same drive to get to know God through His Word and that same yearning to have a relationship with the One who will love you better than anyone on this earth can!

Turn From Your Wicked Ways
The late poet and author Maya Angelou once said, "When you know better, you do better." This holds true for what comes next after you seek God's face. When you learn how God wants you to live your life and how to treat people, then it's time to turn from your wicked ways and do what is good in His sight. Turning away from sin is turning toward God. By turning toward God, you demonstrate that you know and understand God's Word, you accept His unwavering love and you are grateful for His grace and mercy.

Now, just because you turn from your old ways and habits, it doesn't mean you won't still have a struggle between what your flesh wants you to do and what God wants you to do. Even the strongest Christians struggle with temptations daily. Christianity is not about being perfect, contrary to what the world thinks of us. It's about *striving* to do right. People try to hold us to a standard of perfection, then call us hypocrites when we fall short. That word makes me cringe, especially when used by people who have never even opened a Bible!

The Rev. Dr. Damone Paul Johnson from Metropolitan NTM Baptist Church in Albany, New York, once said: "The main problem with humans is sin. That's why we need a savior. And, that's why we need forgiveness." We know we're not perfect. Jesus Christ was the only perfect man, and we will never reach that...EVER! But, because He died for us, sacrificed His life to save ours, then rose from the dead with all power in His hands, we can go to God and ask for forgiveness each time we make a mistake! Thank you, Jesus!

So, Deborah, begin to shed your guilt like layers of winter clothing, because God's gift of forgiveness is available to you!

FORGIVING YOURSELF

Deborah, there have been instances in my life where I have said something or done something that I've regretted. And, because of those regrets, I would sometimes kick myself, punishing myself over and over. Just recently, I had a conversation with someone and I said to her, "I don't know why I ever put a relaxer in my hair to straighten it! My natural hair texture is sooo much better! I forgot that I had beautiful, naturally curly hair!" I first started getting relaxers when I was 13 years old, but I've been chemical free for eight years now. The long, silky tresses looked nice and were easier to maintain, but I endured years of chemical burns on my scalp that turned into scabs, dry flakes and eventually thinning.

It wouldn't be the first time I had that conversation. I've played that same tape over and over when speaking to others about how chemicals are bad and natural is good. And, each time, I would feel horrible for my mistake so long ago.

One of the important lessons in this forgiveness journey is self-forgiveness. After God forgives you, it is then time to forgive yourself. It's easy to beat yourself up time after time when you remember your mistakes. Even worse, when *others* remind you of your mistakes! But if God said in His Word that He would forgive our wickedness and remember our sins no more (Hebrews 8:12) why should we keep rehearsing them in our head? I can't do anything about my past decision to put a relaxer in my hair. I can only move forward and not make the same mistakes of my past.

Remembering your past mistakes can be refreshing when you're looking back over your life to see how far God has brought you. It's praise worthy to note how He kept you even in dangerous situations. And, it's worth marveling at how he gave you what you didn't deserve and kept you from what you did deserve! These are all wonderful testimonies! However, remembering the past becomes unhealthy when it turns into guilt.

Guilt can sometimes make you think you don't deserve forgiveness. This can manifest into lashing out at others, disconnecting from your family or the people you have hurt, deteriorating your mental and spiritual health, returning to destructive behaviors or even suicide. Don't let your past keep you from receiving forgiveness.

I challenge you, Deborah, to examine yourself to see if you are holding on to any guilt or shame. Then, ask God to remove that guilt and have compassion on you.

> *"You will again have compassion on us;*
> *you will tread our sins underfoot*
> *and hurl all our iniquities into the depths of the sea."* - Micah 7:19 NIV

FORGIVING OTHERS

The hardest part of forgiveness is, undoubtedly, forgiving others. I think anyone who has ever been wronged would agree wholeheartedly with me. It's a real struggle! After all, we live in a world where our laws say you must be punished for your offenses. You must stand in court while the judge and jury execute justice based on the severity of what you've done. For example, if you are caught selling or using illegal drugs, the judge is not going to say, "I forgive you this time. Case dismissed, and have a great day!" No, she will impose the fine amount or length of jail time the law allows. Just as people are punished for violating the laws that are set, the carnal side in us wants to punish those who have violated us in some way. That is the world's way. God's way is different. The world calls for justice, but God calls for mercy.

Deborah, I believe you are among those who have a hard time forgiving others. I say this because the letters you've written to me and others over the years were filled with hatred, finger pointing, vile language, and talk of getting revenge on those you say have wronged you.

You even wrote a letter while in jail to my father on December 10, 1998 and told him you had no intentions on speaking to me for the rest of your life. Keep in mind, I was only 24 at the time. You were upset because my youngest sister, who was in Mom's care, went to live with a cousin after Mom died. You didn't appreciate me accompanying her to family court when I went to explain to the judge how she essentially became orphaned just a few short months earlier.

You threatened that same cousin by saying you were going to give someone "a few rocks" to harm her, all because you did not want your children in her care.

While you blamed everyone for the reason why you did not rear your own children, you especially spewed hatred for my brother's paternal family and vowed that they would "get theirs" for lying on you to get him in the first place.

The Gift of Forgiveness

The human side of you taps into your memory bank, and, all those offenses you say people committed against you in the past come rushing into your brain like a tsunami. Once those thoughts enter your mind, they then poison your heart and manifest into awful language and actions.

But the Bible tells you to guard your heart because everything you do flows from it. Keep your mouth free of perversity; keep corrupt talk far from your lips (Proverbs 4:23-24).

Deborah, what happens when you let go of your carnal or human side and start dealing with forgiving others spiritually? You begin to handle situations God's way, that's what! This takes a whole new level of strength, restraint, maturity, prayer and more prayer! But it is possible. Let me share with you how to do this and why it is one of the most important practices you need to incorporate into your life.

Earlier, I mentioned prayer. If you don't pray, or if you don't pray often, you should. I also mentioned the model prayer that Jesus taught His disciples. In that model prayer, He didn't just say pray to God and ask Him to forgive you for your sins. He also said forgive others that sin against you as well! It's a two-way street!

Most Christians may have the model prayer memorized, but I wonder how many people stop reading after the *amen*. Beyond that very simple, yet critical prayer Jesus taught His disciples in Matthew 6:9-13, He goes on to say what I believe are the most important words relating to this topic. Check out these words that follow:

> *"For if you forgive other people when they sin against you, your heavenly Father will also forgive you. But if you do not forgive others their sins, your Father will not forgive your sins."*
> – Matthew 6:14-15 NIV

In other words, if you are holding on to hurt, anger and bitterness to the point where it causes you to not forgive someone, God will not forgive you of your sins! Now that's deep! Did you ever think you could be blocking your own blessings God has for you because of your unwillingness to forgive, Deborah? You could be standing in your own way and not even realize it!

You can't go to God and beg for forgiveness when you are holding on to grudges. That is kind of selfish, don't you think? I don't believe God wants us to prop ourselves up so much with a false belief that we *deserve* forgiveness and no one else does. When God forgives us, it is because of His grace. He shows us favor that we can never earn because we are so flawed. He also forgives us because He loves us; so much, in fact, that He sent His only son into the world to take the place of our sins so that we can have eternal life (John 3:16). We cannot dish out justice to others, while expecting mercy for ourselves.

I hope you see, Deborah, that unforgiveness hurts *you* more than it hurts the person you refuse to forgive. Not only does it cause God to not forgive you when you mess up, but all that hardness and worry can cause stress which leads to physical, emotional and spiritual pain. You are carrying a weight when others have moved on with their lives. You lay awake at night with your body tensed up and your mind racing, when your offenders are planning their next vacation, barely remembering any encounter with you.

Don't lay awake at night plotting your revenge. God will handle that. Don't feel like you always have to give someone a piece of your mind or use curse words to get your point across. Cutting someone down with your tongue will never improve a tense situation. Instead, strive to live in peace. The book of Romans puts it this way:

> *"Never pay back evil with more evil. Do things in such a way that everyone can see you are honorable. Do all that you can to live in peace with everyone. Dear friends, never take revenge. Leave that to the righteous anger of God. For the Scripture says, 'I will take revenge; I will pay them back.' Says the LORD."* - Romans 12:17-19 NLT

Deborah, not only do you want God to forgive you mercifully while you're carrying unforgiveness in your heart, but you also want others to forgive you as well. No, you *expect* them to! It is insulting when you turn your back on your children, then lash out at us because we don't call you Mama or react to you from a place of pain and abandonment. You have hurt us deeply. At some point in our lives, we all have felt unwanted, unloved and vulnerable. We've experienced confusion, neglect and sadness. We've been lost, powerless and disrespected.

Over the years, you have approached us all and have demanded respect because you've merely given birth to us, but you have not respected us or examined the effects your absence and actions have caused in our lives. You have quoted the Bible as a way of making *us* feel guilty by saying, "Honor your father and your mother, that your days may be long upon the land."

If you want friends and family, including your children, to forgive you for your past, start with a simple apology. Go humbly to those you have hurt; not with arrogance, conditions or threats. Leave the "buts" out of the conversation. You know those "buts" you tend to use; "I'm sorry that I wasn't there for you, *but* your grandmother made me mad so I didn't come around." "I'm sorry I didn't raise you, *but* it was all someone else's fault because they lied to the authorities and said I was a bad person." "I'm sorry I stole from you, *but* I had no choice." "I'm sorry I hurt you, *but* I was hurting too."

The "buts" are justifications, but when you are truly remorseful, you don't justify your actions. Also, an apology can't be because you want something in return. You can't apologize only because you need money. That would be a con. Offer a genuine apology even if the other person doesn't forgive you right away. If they don't, then that would be on them to reconcile with God, but you will be freeing yourself from guilt, ushering in peace of mind and making room for God to bless you.

The Gift of Forgiveness

I had a high school classmate who understood the power of "I'm sorry." After graduation, nearly 20 years later, she reached out to me on Facebook. I was new to social media at the time and was connecting with several classmates from my past. She sent me a message in my inbox, and this is what it said:

> *"Hi Lisa. I just wanted to apologize to you for my adolescent behavior back in high school. I'm raising a teenage daughter now & I want her to do well & establish good friendships. So I felt I should practice what I preach & hopefully you are past my foolishness as well, lol. Take care."*

I responded by letting her know I forgive her. And, I offered her an apology for anything I may have said or done to her that was offensive and hurtful. Her response was, "Thank You! It is so freeing to be forgiven."

Deborah, because of the power of "I'm sorry" you can free yourself, let your mind be at ease, and set an example for others who are around you, just as my high school classmate did!

Do you know how to tell if you have truly forgiven someone? When you reach deep down within your soul to forgive someone, you will then be able to pray for them, wish them well, celebrate in their good times, and cry when they hurt. My advice to you is this: forgive, so that you can be forgiven. Let it go, then watch God work!

Charles Lisa

FORGIVING ME

Throughout my young adult years – late teens to early 20s – I started spending time with my father. You could always find us gathered for summer-time barbeques at the park or beach. It seemed like I was meeting a different sibling at every gathering! I think it was my first time going to Beaver Island State Park with him when I realized I had seasonal allergies. My sneezing was non-stop, and there was no Claritin in sight! My small, 95-pound frame was no match for the towering trees and grass beneath my feet in the picnic area. The pollen consumed me. Though somewhat miserable, I still enjoyed those summer days. These are my favorite memories of my time with him.

Then, there were the impromptu gatherings at my father's house. I would be over there playing darts in his living room, while others drank endless amounts of beer. He always made sure he had a wine cooler on hand for a lightweight like me! Friends and family were always dropping in, as I did.

He introduced me to several of his long-time friends as they stopped by. Apparently, some of them knew you too! His introductions always went something like this, "This is my daughter Charles Lisa, you know, Debbie's daughter!" I would roll my eyes so hard I thought they would get stuck! No, I did not want to be labeled as Debbie's daughter! Those words stirred up an adverse reaction. See, I viewed that as a negative connotation. To me, them knowing I was Debbie's daughter meant they knew you were a prostitute. Within that moment, I would ask myself, "Were his male friends men you slept with? Were his female friends women you worked the corners with?" Them knowing I was Debbie's daughter meant they knew of your drug abuse and criminal history. Again, inquiring within, "Do they think I'm just like you, now that they know my pedigree?" Grappling with those thoughts, I would chime in with some comment about not wanting to be associated with you. I was ashamed to be Debbie's daughter. Period.

As I got older, I had to examine that shame and my reactions to people who found out I was Debbie's daughter. Through my journey, I have discovered that I was using judgment that caused me to be uncomfortable at the mention of your name. And, as a Christian, I have also discovered that judging others is wrong.

The Bible explains it far better than I can:

> *"You may think you can condemn such people, but you are just as bad, and you have no excuse! When you say they are wicked and should be punished, you are condemning yourself, for you who judge others do these very same things. And we know that God, in His justice, will punish anyone who does such things. Since you judge others for doing these things, why do you think*

Charles Lisa

you can avoid God's judgment when you do the same things?" - Romans 2:1-3 NLT

That Scripture is an eye-opener for me. Yes, you have done acts in your past that were not pleasing to God. The reality is, so have I. Now, I might not do exactly what you do or did, but God looks at all sin as sin! As a matter of fact, there are none who are righteous, and we all have sinned and come short of the glory of God (Romans 3:23).

Judging others, just like unforgiveness, has its consequences. Jesus warns us not to judge others so that judgement can pass *us* by. And, if we do judge others, God will use that same measuring stick to judge us (Matthew 7:1). That's a severe consequence for my disobedience! I certainly don't want to be a recipient of God's righteous anger!

Don't get me wrong, I can still be displeased, disappointed and hurt by your actions that don't line up with God's Word, while refraining from judging you for those actions. No, I didn't like it when you neglected me, stole from me, broke into my house, talked down to me, called me names, embarrassed me, etc. However, it is not my place to determine your eternal fate based on your actions. I don't have the authority to send you to hell to punish you for your sins. And, I should not think that highly of myself to classify your sins as greater than mine. God calls us to show compassion for one another: "Bear with each other and forgive one another if any of you has a grievance against someone. Forgive as the Lord forgave you" (Colossians 3:13 NIV). This is especially important since I know I disappoint God all the time, and I seek compassion from Him!

Deborah, regardless of what your sins are or how bad they seem to be to others, history tells me that God can use *anybody* to do great things. The Bible demonstrates this through a prostitute named Rahab. She showed kindness to the two men Joshua sent to spy on the land around Jericho that the children of Israel were to possess, because she believed in all she had heard about how great the God of the Israelites were. Rahab hid the men, keeping them out of danger as they were being pursued by men sent by the king of Jericho. In return, when the Israelites conquered Jericho, they spared Rahab and her family (Joshua 6:17).

God used a prostitute named Rahab to help carry out His work. Her story is so significant in the Old Testament that she is listed among a select few in the New Testament who were considered faithful (Hebrews 11:4-31). However, the most fascinating fact about Rahab, in my opinion, is that Jesus is a descendant of hers (Matthew 1:5)!

Yes, Jesus *also* had a prostitute in His family tree! Unlike me, Jesus chose compassion, kindness, mercy and forgiveness when dealing with prostitutes and others that were rejected by society. I often remind myself of

His words when He said, "Do not judge, and you will not be judged. Do not condemn, and you will not be condemned. Forgive, and you will be forgiven (Luke 6:37 - NIV)."

Because I am a sinner, I cannot throw the first, second or third stone, so I'm going to lay my stones down. Deborah, I apologize for judging you for your faults, and I ask that you forgive me, just as I ask God daily to forgive me for my sins.

> *"Do not judge others, and you will not be judged. For you will be treated as you treat others. The standard you use in judging is the standard by which you will be judged. And why worry about a speck in your friend's eye when you have a log in your own? How can you think of saying to your friend, 'Let me help you get rid of that speck in your eye,' when you can't see past the log in your own eye? Hypocrite! First get rid of the log in your own eye; then you will see well enough to deal with the speck in your friend's eye."* - Matthew 7:1-5 NLT

The Gift of Forgiveness

FORGIVING YOU

Deborah, although my few interactions with you in my youth were negative experiences, there were intermittent periods of laughter. As a little girl, I enjoyed seeing the fun-loving side of you. Mom's taste for nice furniture included one of those vintage record player cabinets. One day, you were at our house, and we were playing music on that record player. We mostly played music on weekends or holidays when we had company. You were singing, dancing, laughing and snapping your figures to whatever tunes were hit records at the time. Today, if I hear the song *Bad Boy/Having a Party*, I think of you. Back then, you and Luther Vandross could have a party all by yourselves when that song played! Children just want to laugh, have fun and feel safe. For that reason, this is my most positive memory of you.

I often look back over my life and reflect on my upbringing. I think about how mean and unfair I thought Mom was because I wasn't allowed to go to sleepovers or even visit friends at their houses. I got many whippings with the extension cord, especially when Mom couldn't find Tracy and me because we sneaked over to our friend Tasha's house around the corner (She had the coolest toys)! I reflect on how I was scolded for walking to the corner store without permission with the man next door who bought me a lollipop. And, how I could only play in the front or backyard and had to be in the house when the street lights came on. Then, there were all the whippings I got for not wearing a slip under my school uniform. Apparently my checkered, Catholic school skirts were see through. As an adult now with knowledge of how evil the world can be, with sexual predators lurking around every corner and having reared a daughter of my own, I realize that Mom, in her own way, wasn't trying to be mean at all; she was being protective.

It took a negative encounter with an ex and an emotional experience for me to fully understand this. About 16 years ago, I got into a heated argument with the guy I was dating at the time. He wasn't the neatest guy in the world (that's an understatement), and I was tired of having the conversation with him over and over about him picking up after himself. Tensions were already high as they often were, and I'm sure we had just finished arguing about something else. But this time was different. It got personal. It got nasty. Frustrated because he wouldn't take out the garbage or help me clean, I yelled, *"WHY DIDN'T YOUR MOTHER EVER TEACH YOU HOW TO CLEAN UP AFTER YOURSELF?"* To that he replied, *"AT LEAST MY MOTHER WANTED ME!"* Talk about a dagger to the heart! That was the worst thing anyone had ever said to me. In my mind, though, he was right, which is why those words were so hurtful.

Emotional after hearing those painful words, the best thing for me to do in that moment was to walk away. I retreated to the bedroom to watch TV. Flipping through the channels, I found a movie titled *"Holiday Heart"* starring Ving Rhames and Alfre Woodard. I had never heard of it before, but it didn't matter. I was just looking for some mindless television to take my thoughts off what just transpired.

The Gift of Forgiveness

"Holiday Heart" is about a gay man named Holiday who took a recovering drug addict named Wanda and her young daughter Nicki in to live in his duplex after Wanda was beaten by her boyfriend. Wanda was a single mother who enjoyed writing, and she had aspirations of writing a book about her life's story of overcoming addiction. Nicki adored her mother even though she was a constant victim of Wanda's struggles – lack of stability, revolving door of men in and out of her life, homelessness, target of her mother's theft, etc. Wanda abandoned Nicki after returning to drug use. She was in the apartment alone for two days before Holiday even knew that Wanda was gone. This is when Holiday knew he had to step up to take care of Nicki.

As I watched "Holiday Heart" with extreme interest that day, the theme of a single mother with a young daughter struggling with drug addiction hit close to home and was sobering, especially given the harsh words I had just heard during that awful argument.

The movie sent me on an emotional roller coaster after I saw the most disturbing part of all. Nicki wandered off into the streets, roaming through drug-infested neighborhoods, searching for the mother she loved so much. When she finally found her, Wanda was in a drug house performing sexual acts with strangers in exchange for drugs. She tried to send Nicki away, but Nicki didn't want to leave without her mother. When Wanda's drug-pushing pimp realized this beautiful, preteen was Wanda's daughter, he offered Wanda drugs in exchange for Nicki. Struggling with the demons within, Wanda caved and told Nicki in a desperate voice, "He just wants to kiss you." Nicki escaped the danger that was before her by running off.

Seeing that scene play out of how this strung-out mother was willing to sell her daughter so that grown men could use her for their sexual pleasure made me not only weep uncontrollably, but it made me realize that I was blessed to have not been reared by you, Deborah. I played those words again in my head, "At least my mother wanted me," and I said to myself, "I'M GLAD MY MOTHER DIDN'T WANT ME!" Knowing the danger I could have faced if you would have tried to rear me under your circumstances, made me appreciate the great sacrifices my grandmother - who I once thought was old-fashioned, mean and just too old - made when she took me in. All her rules and "meanness" made more sense as I got older.

Yes, as a child, I wondered why you weren't around much, just as Nicki did in the movie. Holiday said it best though, one day, as he tried to calm Nicki's anger when she questioned why her mother left her, *"Sometimes leaving is the best way to show someone how much you really do love them. Especially if they can't give you what you need."* Suddenly, abandonment didn't feel like abandonment anymore. It felt more like love.

Deborah, the last letter I received from you was on December 18, 2008. Still in jail, you were about 10 years into a 15-year sentence. It's the most memorable one because, for the first time in my life, you offered a *sincere* apology to me for all your trespasses. You not only apologized, but you took ownership of your faults and acknowledged that it was *your* poor choices that

The Gift of Forgiveness

kept you from having a relationship with your children. This long-awaited apology came exactly 10 years after that infamous family court scene where you were cursing me out as the court officers dragged you away in handcuffs.

Throughout the years, and especially after receiving that last letter, I examined this whole notion of forgiving you. I've done it so many times in the past, only to be let down again. It was just easier to not deal with you, rather than risk getting burnt again. After all, how many times should I keep forgiving you when history tells me you will keep repeating the same actions?

As I ponder this question, I am reminded of a sermon Pastor William Gillison Sr. from Mt. Olive Baptist Church in Buffalo preached around 2000. He talked about the story in the Bible where the apostle Peter asked Jesus how often should he forgive someone who sinned against him. "Seven times?" Peter inquired. "No, not seven times," Jesus replied, "but seventy times seven (Matthew 18:21)!"

Jesus continued by telling Peter a parable about an unmerciful servant. This servant owed the king 10,000 bags of gold, but was not able to repay it. The king ordered the servant, his family and all his possessions to be sold to repay the debt. The servant begged the king for more time, so the king showed him mercy by canceling his debt.

The story continues when the servant runs into someone who owes *him* 100 silver coins. He doesn't show him the same kindness that he had just received from the king. Instead, he physically assaults him, then has him thrown into prison until he could pay his debt. When the king found out about this, he reverses his decision and sends him to prison because he did not show compassion and forgiveness to his fellow servant.

In this teaching, Jesus demonstrates how our heavenly Father will treat us if we refuse to forgive our brothers and sisters from the heart (Matthew 18:23-35). When Jesus said seventy times seven, he wasn't prescribing a maximum number of times to forgive someone. He doesn't intend for us to stop forgiving someone after 490 offenses. Instead, he calls us to show unrelenting, genuine compassion and love for others, just as He shows us daily.

My biggest issue isn't whether or not I should forgive you, Deborah. God is very clear in His Word on where He stands with that, as indicated in the many Scriptures I've shared. And besides, since I know what if feels like to be forgiven, I know how to forgive. The difficulty for me is trust. I'll say to myself, "I forgive her, *but* will she steal from me again? I forgive her, *but* is she still on drugs? I forgive her, *but* is she still trying to con everyone around her for financial gain? I forgive her, *but* has she changed?"

I, of course, have legitimate cause for concern. After all, I have not seen you in about 19 years. I barely knew you then, and I know even less about you now. The memories I have of you from long ago aren't good ones. I can't suppress them – as you can see from my clear recollection – so it's difficult to trust you. To trust is to be vulnerable. To be vulnerable is to expose my heart to inevitable pain. The risk of pain causes a wall to go up. As Pastor Damone Paul Johnson once said during a lesson he taught on this topic, forgiveness doesn't mean you don't ever think about it again. It means that it no longer causes a barrier between you and someone!

So, what happens when that wall comes down? When you remove the barrier? The answer is in the book of Proverbs: "Love prospers when a fault is forgiven, but dwelling on it separates close friends (Proverbs 17:9 NLT)." And if I might take the liberty to add, it separates close relatives too!

Growing up in the care of my grandmother was a gift from God. I learned so much from her. I watched her sew many times. I think about that influence every time I pull out my sewing machine to showcase my skills with the needle and thread. I *reluctantly* gardened with her. I reflect on those days in the yard whenever I *cheerfully* reap the harvest from my own garden. I involuntarily helped re-stain kitchen cabinets, laid tile in the kitchen and bathroom, hung wallpaper, and painted. If she were alive, she would be so happy to know how much I love home improvement projects now! After endless road trips to Louisiana every year, my favorite travel method now is by car, much to my husband's dismay!

I watched my grandmother do all that she did equipped with just one arm and the strength God gave her to make it through. Although I gained so much from my upbringing, there was one thing missing – you. I don't want to go back in time. I'm not looking for you to play Mommy. Rather, I desire to have you in my life as someone I can talk to and confide in. As much as I loved Mom, I couldn't do that with her. I would love for you to be someone who I can engage in hobbies with, travel with, and try new experiences with. And, above all, someone I can pray with.

Having a relationship all starts with trust. Can I trust you? I don't know the answer to that question yet. But, I do know who I *can* trust.

> *"Trust in the LORD and do good. Then you will live safely in the land and prosper."* – Psalm 37:3 NLT

Because I trust in the LORD, I should continue to be me and do good deeds for others regardless of whether you or other people are out to take advantage of me or not. This means I will continue to be generous and caring. If I can give to strangers in need of money and clothing, surely, I can give to my own mother. I will extend my ministry to help you if you want me to. If I can serve on the Home Mission Ministry at church, surely I can share the message of Christ's love and help you get the resources you need to live a productive life. And, if I can befriend other former addicts, I can certainly befriend you. Anything I do for others, I do for Christ anyway, so that He may be glorified. I honor Him by helping people in need.

Throughout this letter, I've highlighted numerous egregious offenses you've committed against me and others. I didn't dredge up all these memories to point out what a bad person you are but to demonstrate how deep God's forgiveness can penetrate our family – if we let it. I wanted to demonstrate how I could forgive you in spite of all you have done. I wanted to encourage you to forgive others the same way you want God and me to forgive you. I wanted to show you how sweeter life could be when you incorporate more grace and less anger.

I also want this message to have a ripple effect throughout our family. How awesome would it be for you and me to serve as examples of how relationships can be restored, friendships can be repaired and spirits can be renewed! Let's create new memories. Happy memories. Memories of you interacting with your granddaughter. Dominique is educated, has entrepreneurial aspirations, and loves to dance, just as you did long ago! Being a single mother wasn't easy for me, but she has grown up to be a remarkable woman.

You have six other grandchildren, all under the age of nine, and perhaps you can help guide them to prevent them from making some of the bad choices you've made. You've always said you wanted to reach back and help young girls to prevent them from turning to the streets. Why not start with your own grandbabies?

I would love for you to meet my husband Mike so you can see how God continues to answer my prayers. God didn't send me my husband until I was 40 years old, but when He did, He gave me everything I desired in a spouse.

Wouldn't it be great if you and all your children sat around a dinner table and had a meal together? This simple display of unity and fellowship is something we've never done before. Or better yet, what if we took a family vacation together? The one and only time we have all been together in the same place was during Mom's funeral. Your children were 24, 15, 10 and 6 years old then. That must change. Hopefully, this letter will be the start of the healing that leads to the restoration our family needs (Joel 2:25).

The Reverend Dr. Martin Luther King, Jr. once said, "He who is devoid of the power to forgive is devoid of the power to love." To me, that means forgiveness and love go hand in hand. Jesus calls us to love our neighbor as ourselves. It's one of His greatest commandments. And, with all His teachings, He also gives us free will to make choices. He doesn't hold a gun to our heads and force us to act or think a certain way. No, He puts the power in our hands. He just gives us guidance on what we ought to do, while laying out the consequences for our actions.

Forgiveness is a choice, Mother, and I choose to forgive you.

ACKNOWLEDGMENTS

I give honor to God who is the head of my life; thanking Him always for His wisdom, knowledge and understanding of the mysteries of the Bible. He has given me the talents and provisions I needed to tackle such a difficult, yet important topic.

God has also chosen my family for me, pre-determining who my parents would be long ago. Just as He told Jeremiah in Chapter 1:5, before He formed me in the womb, He knew me. He knew all that would transpire in my life that would bring me to this place where I would be positioned to write a memoir. So, I thank God for my parents whose lives inspired me to write this book.

I am forever grateful to my late grandmother, Hazel B. Little, the superwoman who reared me since I was six months old. The sacrifices you made for me were not in vain. I have hidden your words of wisdom and teachings in my heart; never to be forgotten. I hope to see you again in heaven someday.

Next, I want to acknowledge my daughter, Dominique, whose very existence is the reason why I persevere through life's obstacles. Being your mother is a testimony, and I am constantly motivated to pursue my dreams and passions to serve as an example for you to follow.

Lastly, I thank my husband, Mike, for your unwavering support through my writing process. You have encouraged me and believed in me every step of the way. Your love has pushed me to completion.

I am humbled to be used by God through my writing, and I pray this book transforms someone's life as it has mine.

ABOUT THE AUTHOR

Charles Lisa is a native of Buffalo, New York. She is a graduate of SUNY Buffalo State with a Bachelor of Arts degree in Public Communication.

Her communications career expands more than 20 years, and it has fueled her passion for writing. "A Product of a Pimp and a Prostitute" is her first published book, however, she has authored numerous articles and op-ed pieces.

Charles Lisa is currently a member of Metropolitan New Testament Mission Baptist Church in Albany, New York where she serves on the Christian Education Team and is vice president of the Home Mission Ministry. She has one adult daughter, Dominique, and she and her husband Mike enjoy traveling, as well as a myriad of outdoor activities.

Stay connected with Charles Lisa!

Website: kingjesuspress.com
E-mail: info@kingjesuspress.com
Facebook: CharlesLisaTheAuthor
Twitter: @READCharlesLisa

www.ingramcontent.com/pod-product-compliance
Lightning Source LLC
Chambersburg PA
CBHW020424010526
44118CB00010B/415